Everybody hollering,
"Here come that Peetie Wheatstraw."

I ain't nothing but a hobo,
want somebody to help me carry my load.

Now this is
PEETIE WHEATSTRAW
Well, well, now,
the next time you see me, I'll be
THE DEVIL'S SON-IN-LAW

Blues is a peculiar thing,
they forever on my mind.

I am Peetie Wheatstraw,
the High Sheriff from Hell.
The way I strut my stuff,
oooh, well, now,
you never can tell.

Everybody wondering
what that Peetie Wheatstraw do.
'Cause every time you hear him,
he's coming out with something new.

CHARLES H. KERR
Established 1886

Peetie Wheatstraw, the Devil's Son-in-Law, and High Sheriff from Hell.
(This is the only known photograph of the artist.)

Now I am a man that everybody knows.
And you can see a crowd everywhere he goes.

My name is Peetie, I'm on the line, you bet.
I got something new that I ain't never told you yet.

PAUL GARON

THE DEVIL'S SON-IN-LAW

The Story of
PEETIE WHEATSTRAW
& His Songs
Revised & Expanded Edition

CHICAGO
Charles H. Kerr Publishing Company
Established 1886
2003

On the Cover:
Beth Garon: *Peetie at the Piano*

OTHER BOOKS BY PAUL GARON

Rana Mozelle. Cambridge, MA: *Radical America.*
Surrealist Research & Development Monograph Series No. 4. 1972.

Blues & the Poetic Spirit. London: Eddison Press, 1975.
Reissued, New York: Da Capo, 1979.
Revised, expanded edition, San Francisco: City Lights, 1996.

—, and Beth Garon. *Woman with Guitar: Memphis Minnie's Blues.*
New York: Da Capo, 1992.

—, and Franklin and Penelope Rosemont, eds.
*The Forecast Is Hot! Tracts & Other Collective Declarations
of the Surrealist Movement in the United States, 1966-1976.*
Chicago: Black Swan Press, 1997.

This is a revised/expanded edition of a book
originally published by Studio Vista, London, 1971.

© Copyright 2003
Charles H. Kerr Publishing Company, Chicago

ISBN 088286-266-9 (paper)
088286-267-7 (cloth)

Write for our catalog.
CHARLES H. KERR PUBLISHING COMPANY
Established 1886
P. O. Box 914, Chicago IL 60690

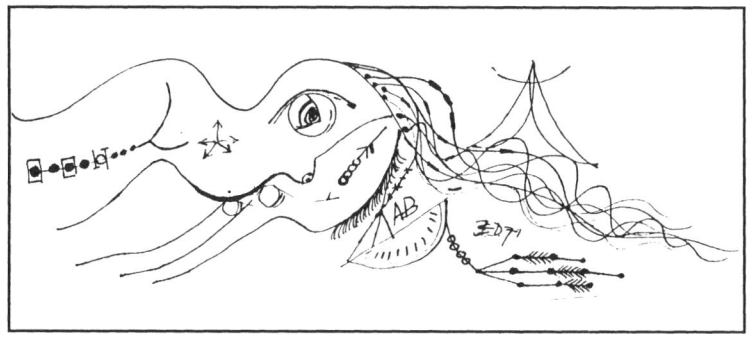

Schlechter Duvall: *Homage to Peetie Wheatstraw— the Man Who Married the Devil's Daughter.*

Table of Contents

Foreword to the First (London, 1971) Edition...........................vii
Introduction to the 2003 Charles H. Kerr Edition.......................ix
The Next Time You See Me
    I'll Be "The Devil's Son-in-Law"...................................1
They Really Used to Like His Way of Playing............................3
He Was Well Known Enough..11
His Real Buddy was Charlie Jordan...14
I Been in the Jungle...35
A Piano Player and a Rounder..56
We Used to Have Luck in the Valley..65
Bring Me Flowers While I'm Living...89
They Came and Said Peetie Was Dead.......................................106
Afterword: So My Evil Spirit
    Won't Hang Around Your Door................................113
Notes..117
Bibliography...119
Discography..122
Index..134

Beth Garon: *Peetie at the Piano*

Foreword to the First Edition

There are several people whose assistance has been invaluable in the preparation of this work. Diane Allmen helped me in all kinds of field work and provided photographic records of every possible item of importance. Her interest in the project provided constant encouragement, and it is to her that I owe my deepest thanks. Mr and Mrs Henry Townsend, Theodore Darby and Joe Williams all gave generously of their time to help piece together Peetie Wheatstraw's story; without their help, there would have been no book. Leroy Pierson not only offered hospitality, but acted as our liaison and navigator in St Louis and East St Louis. His familiarity with the blues scene there enabled us to perform a difficult job with ease. John Simmons read the manuscript and offered many valuable suggestions. To all of the above, I owe my thanks.

I also wish to thank Don Kent, for the loan of his rare Decca catalogue; Yazoo Records, for the superb photograph of Peetie; Erwin Helfer, for his painstaking musical transcription; Jim O'Neal for his research into the circumstances surrounding Peetie's death; and Raeburn Flerlage and Peter Amft for their excellent photographs. Louise Hudson, Franklin and Penelope Rosemont, and Paul Oliver all gave initial encouragement, but it was the latter's pioneering appreciation of Peetie that provided the framework and the inspiration for a full-length study such as this.

I have transcribed all lyrics as accurately as possible, but readers will be able to avoid some confusion if they understand how certain technical problems were handled. Inaudible and undecipherable lyrics are indicated by parentheses, as also are guesses at questionable words and phrases. Although Peetie's 'oooh, well, well' cry is shown in each place where it occurs, numerous difficulties made it impossible to transcribe the phrase in each of its variations. Thus the written transcription 'oooh, well, well' often refers to either 'oooh, well, now' or 'oooh, oooh, well.'

Most of Peetie's verses are of the AAB type, the second line being identical to the first. Although there are often minor variations between the first and second lines of a verse, the second line has not been transcribed unless it differs so radically as to alter the meaning or rhyme scheme established by the first line.

Finally, Peetie's accompanists often recorded under their own names at the session on which they accompanied Peetie. However, when I refer to the number of records made at a certain session, I am only considering the records issued under Peetie's name.

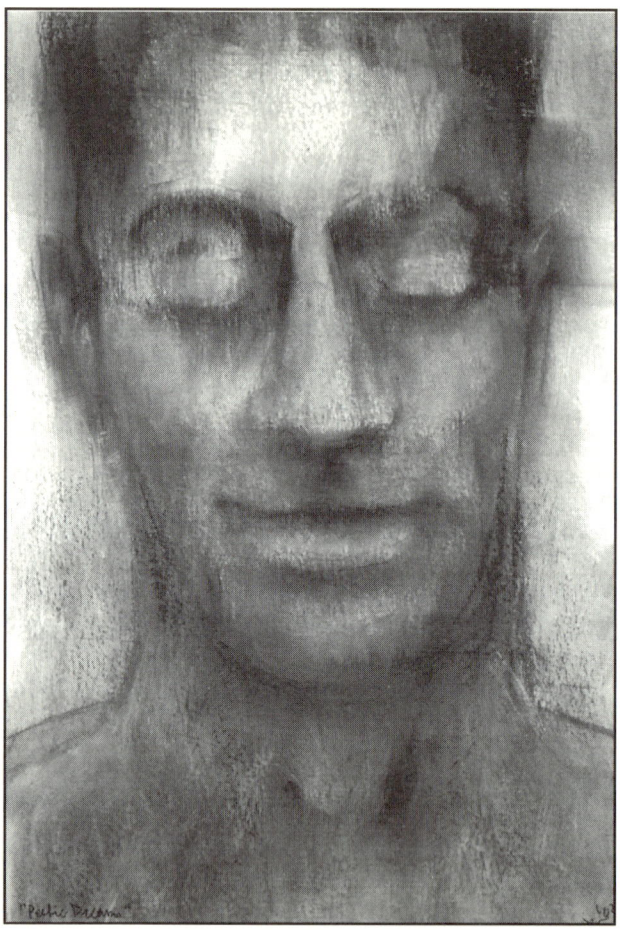

Jen Besemer: *Peetie Dreaming.*

Introduction to the 2003 Edition

When *The Devil's Son-in-Law* was first published in 1971, adding LP appearances to the discography was fairly easy as there were only about 10 LPs to consider. Now there are nearly 100. Certainly from the discographical point of view alone Peetie Wheatstraw's story deserves a new edition. I have added to the discography a separate list of titles of LPs and CDs on which Peetie appears.

Blues appreciation has swelled tremendously in the last thirty years, but it often lacks historical perspective and much attention goes to newer artists. Those who are interested in early blues often restrict their interest to acoustic or slide guitar, and those interested in later blues are often drawn to the electrified Chicago sound. Thirties piano players still aren't the stars on many blues fans' lists. Maybe this book will give fans a closer look at a segment of the blues that they have previously ignored. Some enthusiasts have never heard of Peetie, even though he was one of the most popular blues artists to record in the 1930s.

The first edition is presented here almost intact. I have removed very little material, although a few errors have been corrected, mostly in the lyric transcriptions. I have transcribed and added to the text eight more songs. The St Louis blues scene has given up many more secrets since I was there in 1969, and I have drawn on this research whenever possible. I have cited each of these cases in the text. Since notes were not used in the original edition, the note citations in the text can serve as an informal guide to what has been added. I have expanded the bibliography accordingly.

I have lengthened the section on Ralph Ellison, and the material on Harmon Ray has been extended, also, thanks to the research of Tony Russell. Finally, I have added an entirely new chapter at the end of the book, "So My Evil Spirit Won't Hang Around Your Door." This chapter consists mostly of my own work and speculations.

Most exciting for me are the new illustrations. A number of surrealist colleagues have shared their imaginings of Peetie, and I have tried to choose the best of them to share with the reader. Other blues researchers have been very generous with their discographical knowledge and their names, along with the names of the artists just mentioned, are below.

Gale Ahrens, Görgen Antonsson, Alan Balfour, Jen Besemer, Alasdair Blaazar, Keith Briggs, Carlos Cortez, Schlechter Duvall, Bob Engle, David Evans, Beth Garon, Robert Greenwood, Bob Hall, David Harrison, Sam Lawton, Gary Le Gallant, Eric Leblanc, Wouter Marechal, Luigi Monge, Peter Moody, Jim O'Neal, Jacques Périn, Robert Pruter, Michael Rosas-Walsh, Franklin Rosemont, Penelope Rosemont, Craig Ruskey, Tony Russell, Frank Scott, Chris Smith, Tamara Smith, Paul Swinton, Gene Tomko, Marian and V. Vale, Tony Whetsone, Eliot Williams, and Alan R. Young. R. R. MacLeod's series of lyric transcriptions has also been helpful. Thanks to all of you!

Paul Garon and Vernell Townsend, 1970.

THE DEVIL'S SON-IN-LAW

The Story of
PEETIE WHEATSTRAW
& His Songs

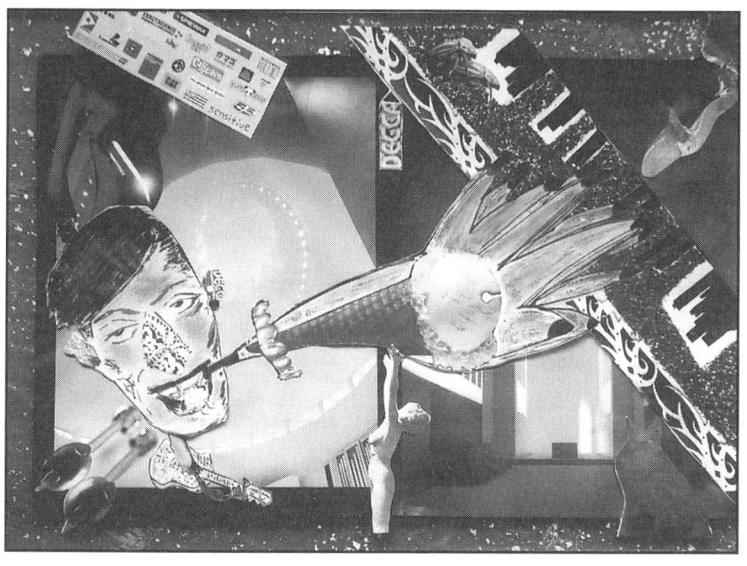

Gale Ahrens: *Peetie's H   Song* (detail)

Penelope Rosemont: *The Return of Akhnaton*:

"The Next Time You See Me I'll Be The Devil's Son-in-Law"

The singer of these words was a man named William Bunch, but to his friends, as well as to an enormous audience of 'race' record buyers, he was known only as Peetie Wheatstraw—the Devil's Son-in-Law, the High Sheriff from Hell. During his eleven-year recording career he made over 160 songs, usually accompanied by his own piano, and provided the accompaniment on countless records by other artists. His style of blues singing was magnetically influential upon all those who came in contact with him or heard his records. It is no exaggeration to say that blues singing in the late 1930s bore the mark of Peetie Wheatstraw.

Yet there can be no "history" of Peetie, in the usual sense. He died over sixty years ago, and the facts we have gleaned give only a thumbnail sketch of his life and personality. We cannot trace his movements at all well, nor even tell for certain where he grew up. His relations are dead or have disappeared, and, although his friends have supplied us with much information, it has been of a fragmentary sort; we still lack a concrete characterization.

This situation, however, has certain compensatory features. There are other ways of finding out about bluesmen and their music, as well as the dynamic conditions which produced them, for the songs themselves constitute a meaningful picture of the blues singer. Blues lyrics reveal an imagination whose forms are contingent not only on experience, but also on desire and aspiration. Although one could no doubt say this of most art forms, what are important and interesting are the very manifestations of imagination in the rich language of the blues. These manifestations, in their various political, social, and cultural contexts, inform the blues with a dynamism seldom found elsewhere. A study like this can provide a rare opportunity to understand the blues singer. We can learn more than we may ever have hoped, not only about the life of the singer, but also about his songs and their significance.

Nonetheless, to many this book will come as a surprise. Even now, when interest in the blues is at its peak, not many people are expecting a full-length study of Peetie Wheatstraw! Yet, as I have implied above, this book is not about Peetie Wheatstraw exclusively; in a real sense, it is about all the blues singers and their songs. Much of the discussion, especially the theoretical material, has a much wider application than its concern with Wheatstraw. Whatever makes Peetie's songs so enduring also attracts us to the blues as a whole. If Peetie had a number of characteristics which bring such qualities into sharper focus, so much the better. That he was an outstanding artist does not in any way make him unrepresentative; indeed, it makes his representativeness more vital, inasmuch as it carries with it so much of the grandeur and eloquence of that whole body of song which we call the blues.

Michael Rosas-Walsh: *Peetie Wheatstraw.*

"They Really Used to Like His Way Of Playing."

William Bunch's application for a social security card, as well as his death certificate, each give 21 December 1902 as his birthdate. But according to US census records, he was born on December 21, 1904, in Ripley, Tennessee, not far from Brownsville. Peetie himself supplied the birth date on the SS-5 application, while his brother Nathan supplied the birthdate that appeared on the death certificate. His father gave the census taker his son William's age as 15 on 6 February 1920. In the 1930 census, on April 15, William Bunch reappears as a "Roomer" at 1012 Jefferson Avenue, 5th Ward, St Louis City, Missouri, aged 25 and single. The informant may have been the landlord Wesley Hooks, who no doubt asked Peetie his age. Peetie's occupation was given as "Laborer, Foundry."

At the present time, we have no more concrete information and no way to reconcile these contradictory dates. Those who follow the theory that information given *closest* to the relevant date is more likely to be accurate will follow the 1904 census date. Those who feel the informant is the most important aspect of the information supplied will be more accepting of the 1902 date.

His parents, James Bunch and Mary (Burns) Bunch moved to Arkansas, where the 1920 census found them on a farm in Freeman Township, about 50 miles Northeast of Little Rock and very close to Cotton Plant. Peetie was the second oldest of seven children: Nathan, the informant on Peetie's death certificate; William (Peetie); Mary L.; Loucretia (sp?); Samuel (who I was to interview in 1970); Lillie Lou; and Will E (sp?), the youngest, aged 9. All were born in Tennessee except a (possible) step-grand-daughter Elinor, aged 3. Peetie's mother was unable to read and write, although he—and his father—could.[1]

When I began work on this book, I could not locate Nathan Bunch to verify the information he supplied. Peetie's widow, Lizzie Bunch, had disappeared The death certificate lists East St Louis, Illinois, as Peetie's residence for the twelve years prior to his death in 1941, so at least we have a rough idea of where he spent his life.

According to Henry Townsend, who was relatively young when he first met Wheatstraw, Peetie could already play piano

Roosevelt Sykes, one of St Louis's great pianists.

Henry Townsend in his home.

and guitar when he appeared in St Louis, probably in the late 1920s. "He was mostly a guitar player in those days, and his piano was pretty much undeveloped," said Townsend. "In St Louis there were so many piano players. It was really a piano town. There were lots of good piano players like Roosevelt Sykes and Henry Brown. And Lee Green, he was much older than all of us—he was a good rag-timer, too." Perhaps it was no accident that St Louis was such a piano town; ragtime had grown up close by, in Sedalia, Missouri.

Teddy Darby added: "We had all kinds of pianos—guitars, too; but we never did have many harmonica players. Now Peetie, he could play guitar or piano, either one." Henry Townsend felt that Peetie's development into an accomplished pianist was nothing unusual. "What I think happened is after he got here, with so many piano players around, he quite naturally leaned toward the piano. It was here that he got to working on his piano playing. 'Course, I wouldn't say that he could play like Sykes and all, but the way Peetie put the words together with his playing, why, I'd say he was as good as anybody around."

If Peetie developed his style in St Louis in the early 1930s, he was certainly exposed to the playing of Sykes, Brown, Green, Stump Johnson, Walter Davis, and many others. Yet none of these men seems to have influenced Peetie's playing. His vocal style and smooth piano technique do call to mind the recordings of Leroy Carr, a tremendously popular artist at that time, and he did influence Peetie, but only in the most general way.

Peetie was well known and respected in the St Louis area. Blind James Brewer remembers him as a "great piano player," adding that "they really used to like his way of playing." St Louis Jimmy never played piano on records because "there were just so many good piano players in St Louis... Peetie Wheatstraw, and Roosevelt, and Steady Roll Johnson and all those guys." Sunnyland Slim recalls that when he came to St Louis in the early 1930s "Peetie Wheatstraw was raisin' sand. Him and Walter Davis was the big names then."

Peetie was not only a big name—he was an original musician who one could recognize anywhere. His "oooh, well, well" cry became such a routine that as Teddy Darby recalls, a woman patron left her chair during one of Peetie's club dates, saying half-seriously, "Good God, why doesn't that man yodel and be done with it?" Peetie's "oooh, well, well" became his trademark,

St Louis Jimmy (James Oden), who wrote or co-wrote half a dozen of Peetie's blues recordings.

but it was hardly his only distinctive trait. The mingling of cries and moans with his half-articulated and slurred lyrics, the characteristic piano figures, and the standard piano introduction all made Peetie easily identifiable.

His lazy and relaxed style of singing could be heard all over St Louis and East St Louis during the 1930s. At clubs like Curly Adams' in Brooklyn—also called 'Lovejoy' after the abolitionist leader and the first all-Black town in the Midwest—on the fringe of East St Louis, or over the barbershop at 1935 W. Biddle Street (now a housing project), one might have heard Peetie, Darby, Townsend, Big Joe, or Peetie's close friend Charlie Jordan. Very few of these artists traveled as much as Big Joe, but one might have seen Darby in Louisville, Kentucky, playing at 18th and Maple, or in Carpet Alley, near the home of Earl McDonald, leader of one of the more famous Louisville jug bands. Although Peetie may have traveled widely, playing first in Louisville, then in Indianapolis, and possibly even in Texas, Big Joe felt that most of Peetie's traveling was done to and from record dates; the rest of the time, said Big Joe, Peetie was in the St Louis area. According to Townsend, Peetie traveled considerably; certainly not as much as Big Joe, who was known as a "real road man," but more than a local figure like Charlie Jordan. Houston Stackhouse recalled seeing Peetie playing guitar in Durant, Mississippi,[2] and Hammie Nixon referred in passing to Peetie Wheatstraw's hoboing from town to town.[3] Darby, who was very close to Peetie, said that they did not travel together, except on an occasional record date.

Darby himself quit playing in the early 1950s, on the death of his friend and piano player, Tommy Webb. He is now [1970] a deacon at the King Solomon Holy House of Prayer, located a few blocks from his Tudor Street home in East St Louis. Born in Henderson, Kentucky, he came to St Louis about 1920, and he has a rich stock of memories of the St Louis blues scene.

When I first began my research for this book, the St Louis and East St Louis scenes seemed to be separate—yet, as more information became available, it became clear that the Mississippi River, which separates Missouri and Illinois, as well as St Louis and East St Louis, was no barrier to the bluesmen, who crossed it constantly during their careers. Thus Peetie, who lived in East St Louis, played in the clubs of the "Valley" district there, while Big Joe, a St Louis resident, might be playing across

Ted Darby in front of his East St Louis home. Darby was one of Peetie's closest friends.

A rare early view of "Deep Morgan," now Delmar Boulevard.

the street from him. Weeks later, both of them could be in St Louis, or perhaps Big Joe would be up in Brooklyn, while Peetie and Darby were playing in St Louis at one of the Biddle Street clubs, not far from the infamous "Deep Morgan", or Morgan Street (now Delmar Boulevard). Some singers probably played and worked north of East St Louis in Alton, while the steel mill town of Granite City doubtless attracted others. The St Louis blues scene, then, was made up of artists from the entire area surrounding St Louis and East St Louis—and all of these artists played in the suburbs and neighboring towns nearly as much as in St Louis itself.

However, one could hardly dismiss East St Louis as a "neighboring town." Its notorious "Valley" district provided steady work for a number of blues singers, as well as for pimps, prostitutes, gamblers, bootleggers, crooked politicians, and assorted hustlers. And of course many of these people, with the exception of the politicians and the slumlords, made their home in the "Valley", as Peetie did.

But East St Louis was not noted for its hospitality to its black residents. Although its 1920 population consisted of nearly 60,000 whites and 7,500 blacks, rumors were spread in early 1917 that the black population had already increased to 15,000–18,000, and that 1,000 blacks were arriving weekly. These exaggerated estimates were utter fabrications, but factory owners and their agents circulated these rumors amidst a white population deeply immersed in strikes and labor conflicts, and the rumors provided vital support to the racist sentiment that was developing in response to the companies' importation of southern black strike-breakers. In July 1917 East St Louis had the worst race riot of the century. The whites murdered at least thirty-nine blacks, partly through the co-operation of the local police and the National Guard. Nine whites lost their lives. Eventually the National Guard remembered the purpose of their presence in East St Louis and began to restore order, but by that time the district had been so torn apart that any real unification of the inhabitants was out of the question. The same racism that precipitated the riot continued to manifest itself at the trials which followed, and judges, juries and prosecutors again discriminated against blacks outrageously Much the same pattern exists in America's courts today, of course, but the riots brought the issue of racism into sharper focus in East St Louis and created a frightening tension that has still not entirely dissolved.

Third Street and the "Valley" in 1970.

"He Was Well Known Enough"

"I can tell you people, you're not going to find any pictures of the 'Valley'—not here, and probably not anywhere. See, that's all gone now, and nobody's proud of it, nobody at all; so there won't be any pictures. I don't care what people say about East St Louis now; there used to be a time when East St Louis was really something. We had classes then, and those people from the 'Valley,' they stayed in the 'Valley.' They didn't come out and mix with everyone like they do now."

A black librarian offered these insights into the atmosphere of East St Louis. Although her main concern seemed to be the degeneration of East St Louis "society," this middle-aged woman was also quite informative on the subject of Peetie Wheatstraw. When I told her I was seeking information on a "blues singer named Peetie Wheatstraw," she continued: "Now I've heard of Peetie Wheatstraw; when I was a little girl, I heard talk of him; he was a piano player. But of course we had nothing to do with people like that. Peetie Wheatstraw, Lonnie Johnson, and all of them—they were from the 'Valley,' you know, and they didn't mix with us. No, you won't find any picture of Peetie Wheatstraw, even in the colored newspaper, not unless he got in trouble. They were a different class; low-life is what they were. That's all. But back before the riot, things were so much different—not like they are now—not at all. Things were so much different then. Nowadays if somebody's a blues singer or something like that, why, his picture would be in the paper with everybody else. But back when Peetie Wheatstraw was around, in the 'Valley,' his picture wouldn't be in the paper unless he got in some kind of trouble. But he was popular, all right. He was well known enough."

Henry Townsend, a keen observer without the class prejudices of the librarian, underlined some if these insights decades later. After noting how important Peetie's death was to the local community, and how St Louis newspapers wouldn't have paid attention to such an "insignificant" fact, he continued: "But if you wanted to find out when he was arrested, you could find that out. They got a record of him on that, I bet you, probably a pretty long one. I bet they got records on him if he did or didn't commit anything. He got arrested plenty. Being a musician, how could you avoid it? They cooked up something on him regardless of what he was doing. Gambling or doing something. They wouldn't just say he's playing music, because there would be no need for them to arrest him."[4]

As our librarian friend said, Peetie was "well known enough." Under the name Peetie Wheatstraw, or, in several instances, "Pete Wheatstraw," he recorded over 160 songs, on eighty-one records, nearly all of them issued. He was one of the more prolifically recorded blues artists, for as well as making his own records he provided the piano (or guitar) accompaniment for many other singers on theirs. These included Charlie Jordan, Kokomo Arnold, Casey Bill Weldon, Jimmie Gordon, Verdi Lee, Mary Harris, Spider Carter, Alice Moore, Leroy Henderson, Barrelhouse Buck McFarland (a singer/pianist with whom Peetie played guitar), and probably others. Peetie and Buck were good friends and often played together. As Henry Townsend remarked, "Around town he was pretty well busy; his name was ringing."[5]

More than one-third of the composer credits on his records were to Peetie himself; one-sixth were to Charlie Jordan, and another one-sixth to "Jordan–Bunch," or vice versa. Jordan's name appeared only once on the Vocalion issues; the rest of his appearances were on Decca. Of the remaining credits, ten were to "Williams," "L. Williams," or "Luther Williams" (all late Deccas), seven to "Harrison," "Harriston," or "M. Harrison," and five to "Smith." There were two credits to "Harrison–Bunch" and three to "Bunch–Smith." Six of the songs were without credits, while Peetie's first record was credited to "Fields–Bunch." Four of the later Deccas were credited to "Giles Jones," and four others to "Oden" (probably St Louis Jimmy); two were to "Green–Oden," and two others to "Green." Two songs were even credited to "Bessie Smith"—possibly to St Louis's Bessie Mae Smith, also called "Blue Belle" and "St Louis Bessie." There was one credit each to "Easton–Bunch," "Muldron Bunch," and "Gordon Bunch," the latter possibly a mis-transcription of "Jordan–Bunch," appearing as it did on the reverse of a title that was credited to "Jordan Bunch." It could also refer to Jimmie Gordon.

Unfortunately, composer credits are not always as significant as they seem. It was common practice to credit an artist with the composition of any song he recorded unless the real composer was well known, or the song was copyrighted. Also, it was not unusual to use composer credits as a way of paying off talent scouts and other artists who were owed money by the recording company. This was a well-established practice, which no doubt accounts for the large number of composer credits to Charlie Jordan, as well as the numerous other unknown names. Jordan was a scout for Decca (and possibly Vocalion) and through him, some musicians have said, Peetie had an opportunity to make records. In any case, Jordan's composer credits probably reflect his ability as an artists' agent more than his talent as a songwriter. Peetie had a great reputation as a composer, and he likely wrote most of his own material, except some of the later songs.

I have tried to confine my discussion of the songs to the presentation of historical information and the suggestion of new approaches to interpretation. I have indicated how I feel certain songs should be analyzed, but I have not said what the results of such an analysis should be; that is left up to the reader. I have, however, attempted to present those songs that offer the sharpest insights into Peetie's life, for it is from them that we can gain the most valuable information.

Peetie played piano on this 1932 recording.

"His Real Buddy Was Charlie Jordan"

On Wednesday, 13 August 1930, when the effects of the depression were being felt more and more strongly throughout the country, Peetie Wheatstraw walked into the Vocalion recording studio in Chicago to make his first records. Although the economic situation made it a very unpromising time for the launching of a recording career, he returned to Chicago five or six more times, and even recorded twice in New York, before April 1932, when his recording activity ceased for two years.

His first recorded songs, released on Vocalion 1552, were duets with a singer called "Neckbones." All the St Louis bluesmen I interviewed remembered "Neckbones", but none of them know his real name. Henry Townsend thought that it might have been "Willie," and, since the composer credit on his record with Peetie reads "Fields-Bunch," his name may have been Willie Fields. On *Four O'Clock In The Morning* "Neckbones" sang two verses and Peetie three. The first song they recorded was the rollicking *Tennessee Peaches Blues* on which "Neckbones" sang the first three verses and Peetie the remaining four.

> N: I was born in Mississippi, raised in Tennessee. (x2)
> But them womens in Missouri picks all over me.
>
> My babe's got something, I don't know what it is. (x2)
> Every time she moves, baby 'n I can't keep still.
>
> Say the peaches I'm loving don't grow on no tree.(x2)
> Lord, it's somewhere, baby, just above your knee.
>
> P: Well, now, you say the peaches you love don't grow on no tree. (x2)
> Well, I believe, now you say, peaches, now, grow just above the knee.
>
> Well, now, I believe I'll go back down in Tennessee. (x2)
> Yeah, baby, now, where the peaches grow, honey, now, just above the knee.
>
> Whoooo, ooooh, well, well, so soon. (x2)
> Well, well, now, oooooo, in your room.

Peaches growing on your knee.
Like the big wild peaches don't grow on no tree.
Well, I believe to my soul, now, down at Tennessee.

    Neckbones's high, thin voice made Peetie's low, rumbling entrance startling, but even without the contrast Peetie's voice was quite distinctive, laced as it was with so many growls, cries, and moans. His piano playing, however, had not developed the individuality that would make him so recognizable four years later. Still, he had a strongly rhythmic left hand, and, although his right was limited, he pursued notes with such a humorously frantic attack that the record is thoroughly pleasant.
    The Vocalion files are rather confusing about the date of Peetie's next four recordings, but it was definitely in the next month or so. The songs were *Don't Feel Welcome Blues,*

Strange Man Blues, School Days and *So Soon,* and on the labels, beneath his name, appeared the words "The Devil's Son-in-Law." This legend appeared beneath his name on almost every record Peetie made; his first record with "Neckbones" was one of the exceptions. The *Don't Feel Welcome Blues / Strange Man Blues* coupling dealt with the "stranger in your town" theme :

> Don't feel welcome in your town anymore. (x2)
> Well, well, now, little mama, baby, now, you drove me from your door.
>
> Ooh, ooh, please, don't drive a good man from your door. (x2)
> Well, well, he may be your best friend, ooh, ooh, mama, you don't know.
>
> Well, well, well, tell me now, little mama, oooh, who can your little man be? (x2)
> Reason, now, I ask so many questions, oooh, oooh, what fault you find of me?
>
> Ooh, let me be your little man, honey, until your big man comes. (x2)
> Well, well, I can do more rolling, now, baby, honey, than your big man ever done.

Strange Man Blues

> Strange man, I just dropped in your town. (x2)
> (I've been a) stranger, please, please don't turn me down.
>
> Well, well, I'm a stranger here, baby, and I'm a long ways from home. (x2)
> Well, well, well, I've been mistreated, now, little mama, oooh, since I been born.
>
> Well, well, mistreat me here, baby, but you can't when I go home. (x2)
> Well, well, well, you mistreat me there, baby, honey, now, you (all) alone.

Well, well, run here, little mama, please sit down on my
  knee. (x2)
Well, well, let me tell you, baby, oooh, oooh, how you
  treated me.

Well, well, well, you treated me dirty, mama, baby, now,
  you treated me mean. (x2)
Well, well, you treated me like, little mama, the man, now,
  you never seen.

One cannot say that Peetie invented the "stranger" theme, since it occurs in many blues prior to these. Tampa Red did much to popularize the song, however, and his *New Stranger's Blues* was recorded about six months *after* Peetie's.

The guitarist at this session was Peetie's close friend Charlie Jordan. Peetie and Jordan played on each other's records for five years and they often worked together outside the studio. "All these people saying they're 'Peetie Wheatstraw's Buddy,' but his real buddy was Charlie Jordan," said Big Joe. "Jordan first got Peetie on records, you know, and he really was his buddy for all the time Peetie was alive." Joe knew Jordan well; for a while, they shared a rehearsal hall on 17th and O'Fallon in St Louis. "We had our own hall, and everybody would come there to rehearse and to meet people to make records. You had to pay dues, thirty-five cents, and everyone was there. You can ask Roosevelt, he'll tell you about our hall; he'll tell you about Jordan, too." Everyone remembered Charlie Jordan, and from a number of stories and anecdotes a few concrete facts emerged. He was an extremely popular St Louis musician who could walk only with crutches. He had a series of strokes towards the end of his life and was partially paralyzed, but, according to Big Joe, he was originally crippled by a bullet in the spine, long before he had his first stroke. Other sources confirmed the bullet-wound, but in the leg. About that time Jordan was involved in bootlegging, and it was then that he was shot. He lived on 8th Street and then on 17th and O'Fallon. Not surprisingly, he traveled very little, and, although it was once rumored that he was shot to death, records at the St Louis Bureau of Vital Statistics indicate that he died of more or less natural causes, either pneumonia or arteriosclerosis. Jordan was with Peetie on 4 November 1930, when they returned to Chicago to make four more songs for Vocalion. *Ain't It A Pity And A Shame* was coupled with *Don't Hang My Clothes On No Barb Wire Line*—both good performances, lyrically as well as musically. *So Long Blues* was rather average, but it was coupled with the growling *Mama's Advice*, probably the. first of Peetie's recorded blues one can call solidly cohesive in theme. If one can use records as a guide, his ability to sing, play, and compose was developing quickly.

Ain't It A Pity and a Shame

(It's) a pity and a shame way some women treat their man. (x2)
Ehh, some of them, now, will take your money, carry it and give it to another man.

(So early) this morning when everything was still (x2)
Well, well, well, I seen my little mama as she come creeping off the hill.

Hmmm, bring me my pistol, shotgun and some shells (x2)
Well, well, now, I've been mistreated, baby, now, I'm gonna raise some hell.

Well, well, have you ever waked up mama between midnight and day? (x2)
Now with your head on the pillow where your good man he once have laid.

Hmmm waked up this morning mama about the break of day.
Ehh crying, know now I mean it.
Waked up this morning, please, about the break of day.
Well, now my little girl she quit me, mama, now, my wife she's gone away.

Don't Hang My Clothes on No Barb Wire Line.

Eh, don't want my clothes hung on no barb wire line. (x2)
Well, well, I won't go crazy, but baby, I'll gradually lose my mind.

Well, well, I don't want no sugar, mama, sprinkled in my tea. (x2)
Well, uh, some of (St Louis) women, they are sweet enough for me.

Well, well, well, I can't use no gravy mixed up in my rice. (x2)
Well, well, well, now, the one I love I believe she can mix it, mama, so nice.

Ohh, little girl got buggish, she throwed all of my clothes outdoors. (x2)
Well, well, honey, now, I wonder, mama, will a shopping bag hold my clothes.

Oooh, wonder do my little girl knows where I am? (x2)
Well, well, now, I wonder do she know that I'm fixing to beat it on back to 'Bam.

He and Jordan returned two months later in January 1931 and Peetie sang *C And A Blues* the first of three versions that. he recorded; it was a typical train blues with a strikingly unusual off-time piano break. The record company rejected its session mate, *Six Weeks Old Blues*, and Peetie and Jordan returned two months later to remake it.

Well, now, now, my mama, she told me when I was only six weeks old. (x2)
She said, "son, now, when you get six weeks old, now, mama gonna set your clothes outdoors."

Well, well, I looked at my mama, baby, and I began to smile. (x2)
Mama, now, good times kill me, true believe your poor boy die.

Sometimes I would weep, then again I would moan like a mourning dove. (x2)
Mama, now, you know, your life not worth living, oooh, well, when you're not with the one you love.

Mama, now, gonna leave here walking, mama, now, gonna pin crepe on my door. (x2)
Mama, now, you know I won't be dead, but now, I'm not coming here no more.

When I die, oooh, well, please bury my body low. (x2)
So, now, that my evil spirit, mama, now, won't hang around your door.

Many of Peetie's more popular Vocalions were released on the Conqueror label as well as on later Vocalions; some were also issued simultaneously on the various ARC labels, but even those that were not re-released, like *Six Weeks Old Blues*. were either popular enough or attractive enough to supply a rich fund of material to other blues singers. For example, John Henry Barbee recorded *Six Weeks Old Blues* eight years later.

In Chicago, on 28 September 1931, Peetie made his only records for Bluebird; the guitarist with him may have been Charlie McCoy. The four performances were rather remarkable. Although the words "The Devil's Son-in-Law" had been appearing below his name on his previous records, there was no such legend on the Bluebirds. Instead, one side of B5451 was titled *Devil's Son-in-Law* and the reverse *Pete Wheatstraw*; Bluebird issued both records as by "Pete Wheatstraw." For Peetie, these records were an important step in his effort to publicize himself as a rather unusual figure, and, although the tone of the lyrics is tame compared with that of the later "stomps," one must consider the Bluebirds a significant part of the foundation of Peetie Wheatstraw's "Devil's Son-in-Law" legend. On *Pete Wheatstraw*, invoking the rather surrealist notion of prowling over the clouds, he sang:

> Now this is Peetie Wheatstraw this morning, people want to know where do I prowl. (x2)
> Some time I prowl in the far distant lands, sometimes I prowl o'r the rising clouds.
>
> Now I once was a good boy, mama, I was good all over town. (x2)
> Well, well, now I don't see why people try to throw me down.
> When I first met you, little baby, baby, this is the lie you told. (x2)
> You said, "Now you can get my money, baby, honey", and I will be made of silver and gold.
>
> [spoken] What you gonna do, Charlie? You gonna play it for a minute?
>
> Now, what you gonna do, little mama, when your road gets dogged like mine? (x2)
> Honey, now, you will be worried, mama, now, and bothered all the time.
>
> Now, if anybody asks you, baby, honey, now, who composed this song. (x2)

> Now, now, will you please tell them it was Peetie Wheatstraw, mama, now, he has been here and gone:

Devil's Son-in-Law contained a vivid reference to rattlesnakes, a recurrent symbol in Wheatstraw's blues.

> Now where would you be, mama, baby, now, you made my life a wreck. (x2)
> I'd rather have a rattlesnake, honey, now, wrapped around my neck.
>
> When you used to love me, now, little mama, it would go clear down through my toes. (x2)
> Well, well, now, the way that I loved you, mama, honey, now, don't nobody know.
>
> Now I got eleven women, and I got one little indian squaw. (x2)
> Well, well, now, the next time you see me, I'll be the Devil's Son-in-Law.
>
> [spoken] Play it for me one time; pick it now, boy.
>
> Now if you take my little woman, you can't keep her long. (x2)
> Well, well, now she will coming running home, crying, "Daddy, I done wrong."

In a later chapter, I discuss more thoroughly Wheatstraw's maintenance of this awesome identity, but even at this early stage certain features become clear. The vitality of spirit that was manifest in his poetic elevation of his own self-image was a tremendously important factor in his popularity. This poetic form of protest was a hundred times more powerful than the "protest songs" which meant very little to the average black worker. To be Peetie Wheatstraw, the Devil's Son-in-Law, was to be much more than a member of the black working class could ever be in white capitalist America. And to be the Devil's Son-in-Law was to initiate a poetic motive force in the direction of freedom and liberation that has been all but ignored in current analyses of the blues. As our discussion of Peetie's songs continues, gaining insight into this phenomenon will become easier.

Peetie's other Bluebird coupling was *Creeping Blues* and *Ice And Snow Blues*; the fourth verse of the latter contained a graphic, violent image, a foretaste of the violence that figured more prominently in his later songs.

> This winter, baby, in the ice and snow,
> You know, my little mama gon' be sleeping on her floor.
> Baby, now, you know you got to reap, baby,
> Just what, what you sow.
>
> You remember last winter, you drove me from your door,
> Now, little mama, it was in the ice and snow.
> [refrain]
>
> You left me, baby, because I was cold in hand,
> You taken my money, and spent it on your other man.
> [refrain]
>
> I did more for you than you understand,
> You can tell by the bullet-holes, mama, now, here in my hand.
> [refrain]

In March 1932 Peetie went to New York to record four new songs for Vocalion. He made *Police Station Blues* and *All Alone Blues* on 15 March and *Can't See Blues* and *Sleepless Nights Blues* on 17 March, accompanying himself only with his peculiar guitar playing. I have always preferred Peetie's piano to his guitar, which seems much too jerky, but many people favor his guitar work. Henry Townsend and Teddy Darby, for instance, both guitarists, liked Peetie as guitar-player rather than a pianist. Big Joe Williams, however, held the opposite view. "Peetie never was much of a guitar player; could play a few things and was good on those little things, but that's all. But lemme tell you, he was one hell of a piano player."

Police Station Blues

> Well oh well, mama, now, on some old rainy day. (x2)
> Well, well, now, you're gonna be sorry, ooh, ooh, babe, you walked away.

Well, well, when the sun rose just above the trees. (x2)
Well, now, I went to the police station and asked them, mama, now give me my little girl, please.

Well, now, your days so lonesome, your nights so dreadful long. (x2)
Well, well, there been so many lonesome days, ooh, ooh, well, babe, since I been gone.

Well, well, tomorrow is Sunday, ooh, ooh, well, you may see me Christmas eve.
Crying well, y'know I mean it.
Well, well, tomorrow is Sunday, you may see me Christmas eve.
Well, well, have I got a present, mama, babe, on your Christmas tree?

Baby, now, when are you going to give me, ooh, mama now, the things you promised me.
So unkind, well now, know now I mean it.
Oooh—— things you promised me.
Well now I don't see why, baby, now, you so hard on me

After this session Peetie went unrecorded for two years. When he resumed in March 1934 he had developed a characteristic way of singing and playing that made him instantly recognizable.

Introduction to *Road Tramp Blues*.

Two features especially came to be identified with him: his regular use of the phrase: "oooh, well, well" in the third line of nearly every verse he sang, and his tendency to employ a certain piano phrase to introduce almost every song. The above transcription of the introduction to *Road Tramp Blues* is quite typical.

Apparently Peetie developed his stylistic consistency during the years he went unrecorded, for his 1931–2 sessions do not give any evidence of what was to come in 1934, except in the use of moans and "ooh, well's" scattered through various lines in various places. It would have been interesting to trace this step of Peetie's evolution in detail, but it is impossible since he made no records during this crucial period.

Peetie recorded six songs for Vocalion at his 25 March 1934 session. *My Baby Blues* was never issued, but Vocalion 02783, *Back Door Blues* and *Packin' Up Blues*, was an excellent coupling. Of the three remaining sides, *Midnight Blues, The Last Dime,* and *Long Lonesome Dive*, the first was coupled with a song from a later session, while the other two were coupled on Vocalion 02712, as well as on Conqueror and other ARC labels; on these latter issues, the song was mistitled *Long Lonesome Drive*, as it may have been in the files. A superbly swinging piano, imaginative lyrics and an intensely emotive delivery made *Long Lonesome Dive* one of the best records Peetie ever made. Sadly, one must really hear this record to appreciate it fully:

> Blues is a worst old feeling that will make you feel so bad. (x2)
> Now, you know they're the worst old feeling, oooh, well, well, Lord, that I ever had.
>
> I got a blues so bad that I don't know what to do. (x2)
> (When) you get in trouble like me, little mama, oooh, well, well, you will have them, too.
>
> Blues, now, the blues, blues have got the best of me. (x2)
> Now, I can sit here and wonder, oooh, well, what's gonna become of me.
>
> [spoken] Hard sometime, ain't it?

Vocalion
U.S. PAT. 1,637,544
Not Licensed for Radio Broadcast
02712-A
LONG LONESOME DIVE
Peetie Wheatstraw
(The Devil's Son-in-Law)
Vocal with Guitar and Piano
BRUNSWICK RECORD CORPORATION

> Don't want me, baby, why don't you tell me so? (x2)
> I'm a hypnotizing daddy, I can get me a woman every place I go.
>
> I'm going down to the Mississippi, I believe I'll take me a long lonesome dive. (x2)
> Do you think that if I commit murder, well, God, will I ever get back alive?

Here Peetie uses the word "murder" as a synonym for suicide: If I jump into the Mississippi (the "long lonesome dive"), will my suicide attempt be successful?

Five months later, in August 1934, Peetie made his first records for Decca, the label on which two-thirds of his recorded output was to appear. Musically, the first Deccas were nothing special, but some of the lyrics were intriguing. The first two lines of *Numbers Blues* consisted wholly of "oooh, well, well's," and a humorously sarcastic spoken part punctuates the middle of the song.

> Oooh, well, ooooh, well, oooooh, well [etc.] (x2)
> Numbers on my mind, oooh, well, you know it's hard to tell.
>
> Numbers and horses always on my mind. (x2)
> But, you know, the way that I play them, oooh, well, well, seems like I am blind.
>
> Now I have some numbers, I play 2, 22, and 25. (x2)
> But, now, you know, if I don't catch them numbers, oooh, well, well, I believe, now, that I'll lose my mind.
>
> [spoken] Boys, now, you know, if I was you, I would quit gambling. Do like I do—I let it go. Follow poor me. Gambling is gonna ruin ya. Now a good boy, let's all be the same way, like I am.
>
> Now, you know, I played this game, then again, I played it for a great long time. (x2)
> Said, now, if I don't stop this game, oooh, well, well, I'm going to lose my mind.

The numbers game, or policy, flourished in East St Louis, just as it did in all lower-class areas and slums. (For a full account of the game and its relationship to the blues, I refer the reader to Paul Oliver's *Screening The Blues*.) It is obvious from listening to *Numbers Blues* that the spoken advice was intended to be sarcastic and humorous—and this sort of humor is the kind that one always encounters in the blues, for the blues singer rarely tells jokes in his songs. Rather, the blues singer uses humor as a weapon with which to combat the forces of repression and oppression that surround the blues singers and their audience. As such, it too must be looked at in the light of revolt. "Humor is not resigned," Freud has said, "it is rebellious. It signifies not only the triumph of the ego but also of the pleasure principle, which is able here to assert itself against the unkindness of the real circumstances."

Coupled with *Numbers Blues* was *All Night Long Blues*; it also had a spoken aside, this time more violent than humorous:

> Ain't it hard sometime, when you get in bad luck? Sometime that a man don't know just what to do. But I'm gonna tell you what I'm gonna do for myself. I'm gonna get me one .45. Now, I'll take care of myself then.

Peetie's audience could certainly appreciate the desire for a .45. With a .45 one might gain respect, money, or even a longer life—all things denied to members of the black working class. Also, the wish for violence was an inevitable effect of the frustrations constantly felt by the ghetto residents. Although the listener could identify with the singer in his desire to have a gun and become more powerful, one would be mistaken to label this reaction "escapist" and dismiss it. As we shall see later, the role of fantasy is much more significant.

Peetie made two other songs for Decca that week. *Good Home Blues* and *These Times*. Apart from a startling piano error in the latter, they were not very notable. The next day, 24 August, he was back with a band. Accompanied by Ike Rodger's trombone, Henry Brown's piano, possibly his own guitar, and an unknown clarinet and violin, Peetie whooped and hollered his way through *Throw Me In The Alley*. Perhaps because he had a full band for support, his voice was even stronger than usual. The song had only two verses, and Peetie never sang better.

> ('low), let's go down in this alley.
> Oooh, well, well, let's go down in this alley.
> Peetie Wheatstraw, good people, gonna put you all in the alley.
>
> Bye, bye, baby, what's the matter now?
> Oooh, well, well, what's the matter now ?
> The way you treat me, little mama, you don't mean me no good no how.

Two weeks later he was back with Vocalion. It was the last time he played guitar on record, and indeed he did so on only two of the four songs, *Keyhole Blues* and *Long Time Ago Blues*, the latter containing several oblique references to law and police troubles. On *C And A Train Blues* and *Last Week Blues* he played piano. The lyrics of *Last Week Blues* were certainly absorbing, and they serve as an excellent example of Peetie's original and individual talent. The theme of counting the days was not an unusual one in the blues, but Peetie's treatment of it was entirely his own.

> Last Sunday I had the blues last Sunday night I had (to pay?). (x2)
> Because my woman, she had left me, oooh, well, well, now, don't have no place to stay.
>
> Last (Sunday) she stayed out, now, with her other man. (x2)
> But since she been gone away from home, oooh, well, well, now, she been going from hand to hand.
>
> Last Wednesday, she began to cry. (x2)
> She said, "Daddy, daddy, when I come home, now, I'm coming home to die."
>
> Last Thursday she went out to the camp that was no-man's land. (x2)
> And all the women that was up there, oooh, well, well, now, they's going from man to man.
>
> Last Friday morning, she came back to her old neighborhood. (x2)
> And now, you know, she found out, oooh, well, well, that she couldn't do her own self no good.
>
> Last Saturday night, she began to have them blues. (x2)
> Well, well, now, you know, she said, "Daddy, daddy, oooh, well, well, now, please let me come back home to you!"

C And A Train Blues was Peetie's second version of the song:

> Well, well, let me tell you people what the C and A will do for you. (x2)
> Well, now, it'll take your little woman, oooh, well, well, and blow black smoke back at you.

August-September, 1927

CHICAGO
AND
ALTON
RAILROAD

Time Tables

All Passenger Trains are Operated on Central Standard Time which is One Hour Slower than Chicago Daylight Saving Time

CHICAGO AND ALTON TRAINS ARRIVE AT
AND DEPART FROM
THE NEW UNION STATION
AT CHICAGO

Well, now, I went to the station, and the moon was shining
bright. (x2)
Well, now, I wanted to see my baby, oooh, well, well, but
that ol' C and A was out of sight.

Well, now, I have to see my baby before the sun rise again.
(x2)
Well, now, but I got to be on time, oooh, well, well, now, to
catch that C and A train.

[spoken] Boys, when you ain't seen your girl in a long time,
please do like Peetie Wheatstraw, the Devil's Son-in-Law,
the High Sheriff from Hell. I'm gonna see her before the
sun rise again.

Well, now, I haven't seen my baby, Lord, in I can't tell
when. (x2)
Well, now, you know, I made it up in my mind, oooh, well,
well, to catch me a C and A train.

Well, well, now, I'm leaving town, I'm gonna ride that C
and A train. (x2)
Well, now and I don't know when, oooh, well, well, that
you'll see me back again.

The Chicago and Alton Railroad, later called the Alton Railroad, operated between Kansas City, St Louis, and Chicago, with principal stops at Alton, Springfield, Peoria, Bloomington, and Joliet, all in Illinois. It also served the Missouri towns between Kansas City and St Louis. It offered some of the most luxurious passenger accommodations available anywhere, and it continued to operate until the late '40s, when it was taken over by the GM & O (Gulf, Mobile and Ohio).

Peetie's *C And A Train Blues* is also noteworthy in that here, for the first time, he refers to himself as the "High Sheriff from Hell." Although that nickname only appeared once on a record label, his contemporaries still associate it with him nearly as readily as the more common "Devil's Son-in-Law." Indeed, I spoke to no one who recalled Peetie Wheatstraw without remembering him as the "Devil's Son-in-Law" or the "High Sheriff from Hell." Many of the same people had never heard of William Bunch.

Four days later, on 11 September 1934, Peetie was back with Decca. He made one song, accompanied by his own piano and a guitar, presumably played by Charlie McCoy. Although it was the sixth number he recorded for Decca, the company released it before any of the others; the reverse was by Jimmie Gordon and beneath Gordon's name was the legend "Peetie Wheatstraw's Brother"! Peetie's song was called *Doin' The Best I Can*, and was the first of several songs on the same theme that used the melody made popular by the Mississippi Sheiks' *Sitting On Top Of The World*.

> When a man is out working, working hard on the line,
> Some low-down rascal, always trying to steal his wife,
> But here I am,
> Hard working man,
> Doing the best I can.
>
> I hate to hear New York Central whistle blow,
> Everytime she whistle, to the round-house I got to go.
> [refrain]
>
> I don't know hardly, baby, what to do,
> Don't want to hurt your feelings, either get mad with you.
> [refrain]
>
> You wake up this morning, rag around your head,
> Asked you to cook my breakfast, but you went back to bed.
> [refrain]
>
> Went out this morning, could not make no time,
> Didn't have no blues, but I was all worried in mind.
> [refrain]
>
> I'm a hard working man, and trying to do things just right,
> But my woman she (got) on me, I ain't going to work tonight.
> [refrain]

Little Johnnie Jones was one of a number of artists who recorded this song in the post-war era, often as *Working Man*.

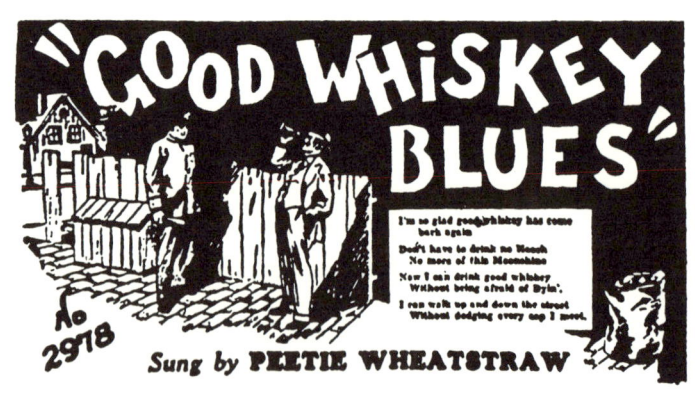

2978—GOOD WHISKEY BLUES and LETTER WRITING BLUES—Vocal—Piano-Guit. Acc. Sung by Peetie Wheatstraw 59c

"I've Been in the Jungle..."

The ratification of the 21st Amendment on 5 December 1933 repealed prohibition which had been in effect since January 1920.

Illicit stills continued to produce bootleg whiskey even after Prohibition was repealed. This one was raided by the St Louis police in September 1934.

Many blues enthusiasts forget that the entire period of vintage blues recording, with all its references to whiskey and drunkenness, took place during an era when liquor was entirely illegal. America had passed a law against its own inner impulses, only to find its impulses stronger than its laws.

Besides provoking a series of well-known reactions like speakeasies, bootlegging, and a marked increase in crime, prohibition also created a huge market for several dangerous alcohol combinations and derivatives, which were frequently drunk by those desperate enough for intoxication at any price. And the price was often very high: consumption of "bad whiskey" frequently led to permanent tremors, paralysis, blindness, and even death. Drinking too much Jamaica Ginger, a flavoring extract, sometimes resulted in a crippling disability that was commonly referred to as "jake leg," and 1920s repertoires contained several blues about that condition.

Peetie's reaction to the legalization of liquor seemed to be profound relief, as detailed in his *Good Whiskey Blues* and *More Good Whiskey Blues*, recorded one day later. In *Good Whiskey Blues*, he sang:

> I'm so glad good whiskey have come back again. (x2)
> Now I can drink my good whiskey, oooh, well, well, also my good Holland gin.
>
> Now I'm so glad I don't have to drink this hooch no more. (x2)
> Well, now, because it killed my pardner, oooh, well, well, and it had me on the killing floor.
>
> Well, now, I'm so glad we got good whiskey back today. (x2)
> Well, now, I can drink all night long, oooh, well, well, I won't have no doctor bill to pay.
>
> Ehhh, now I'm so glad I don't have to drink no more moonshine. (x2)
> Well, now, I can drink my good whiskey, oooh, well, well, and I ain't afraid of dying.
>
> Well, now, I'm so glad that good whiskey can't be beat. (x2)

> Well, I can walk up and down the street, oooh, well, well,
> without dodging every cop I meet.

More Good Whiskey Blues was more of the same :

> I'm so glad good whiskey have made it through. (x2)
> Well, now, it have saved my wife from dying, oooh, well, well, and saved my sweetheart, too.
>
> I'm so glad good whiskey has come back in time. (x2)
> Because, now, I drink so much hooch, oooh, well, well, I'm 'bout to lose my mind.
>
> I'm so glad good whiskey sure is here. (x2)
> Well, well, now, if you can't drink good whiskey, oooh, well, well, why not drink some dog-gone good beer?
>
> I'm so glad good whiskey has come back to me. (x2)
> Well, now, it brought me good things, oooh, well, well, now, from way across the sea.
>
> You is just as welcome, good whiskey, now, as the flowers is in May. (x2)
> Well, since you has come back to me, oooh, well, well, now, I hope you have come to stay.

When Peetie came to the Vocalion studio in Chicago on 25 and 26 March 1935, with him was Casey Bill Weldon. (If there was a second guitar on some of the records made at this session, it was probably played by Teddy Darby, and not Charlie Jordan as has been thought.) Weldon, who may have been the Will Weldon who played with the Memphis Jug Band for a time, made a number of records in the "30s, on which he was described as Casey Bill, the "Hawaiian Guitar Wizard." He played the guitar as it lay across his lap and used a conventional steel slide, with a "Hawaiian" technique, instead of the more common knife-blade or bottleneck slide. According to Big Bill Broonzy, he was born in Pine Bluff, Arkansas, and moved to California some time after making his last records. Big Joe remembered seeing him in California in the early 1950s, but has not encountered him since. His name was unfamiliar to a number of St Louis bluesmen, and he may have lived in Kansas City during the '30s. Big Joe remembered that Casey Bill drove from Kansas City to Chicago to make his records, and several of his records were labeled as by "Kansas City Bill Weldon." The name "Casey Bill" was taken from the abbreviation for Kansas City, K.C.

Personally, I feel that Peetie and Casey Bill never really helped each other. The Casey Bill records on which Peetie played were much stiffer than those which had Black Bob as the pianist, and the Wheatstraw recordings on which Casey Bill played did not have the easy, relaxed atmosphere that was evident when Peetie played with Jordan or, later, Kokomo Arnold. Still, some of the songs are interesting and quotable. *Rising Sun Blues* had a taste of Peetie's growing arrogance.

> She said she had gone away to leave me, and I wondered why don't she stay away. (x2)
> Seems like, now, she ought to have it in her mind, oooh, well, well, that I can get me a girl each and every day.
>
> Well, now, that don't worry me, baby, I have it in my mind that I can go. (x2)
> Well, then again, after I'm gone, oooh, please, now, don't bother with me no more.

Of the other three songs Peetie recorded that week, *Truthful Blues* and *Blues At My Door* were coupled for release.

Blues At My Door

> This morning soon, blues was standing in my door. (x2)
> Please, will you leave here, blues, oooh, please, blues, don't come here no more.
>
> Blues, now, you know they are bad, they keeps me bothered all the time. (x2)
> Now if I don't do something for the blues, oooh, well, well, they gonna make me lose my mind.
>
> Blues is a peculiar thing, they forever on my mind. (x2)
> Then again, if the blues stay with you, my friend, oooh, well, well, they will always have you crying.

> Now, I received a letter, now, from a girlfriend of mine today. (x2)
> She said, now, she could do much better, oooh, well, well, but I was always in her way.
>
> Now, good-bye, blues, please, blues, don't bother me no more. (x2)
> Blues, now, won't you give me a break, oooh, well, well, please now, don't knock on my door.

The device of personification is as well known in traditional poetry as it is in the blues, but the academic standards by which one evaluates traditional poetry cannot sensibly be applied to the blues. For the blues is poetry of another sort, and indeed, it is unusual in the blues to come upon a "traditional" line like this one from *Truthful Blues* "Well, now, you can tell it's autumn, when the leaves begin to fall."

On his next session, for Decca, on 17 July 1935, Peetie was accompanied by his own piano only. Bukka White remembered that the first time he went to Chicago—around 1935—was with Peetie, but he didn't record with him; this could have been that trip.[6] Of the six songs issued, *C And A Train Blues* (number three) and *Good Hustler Blues* (Decca 7123) are both above average. In the latter, he castigates his girlfriend for having "pimps on your brain," ending with the lament, "I believe you got a pimp, oohh, well, well, you give my money to."

Whiskey Head Blues and *Slave Man Blues* were average lyrically, but the accompaniments departed slightly from the routine piano figures that could be heard on most of his other recordings of that period. *Cocktail Man Blues* was his first suggestive or "party" blues. Peetie made proportionately few recordings of this type, and it was to his credit that he always had enough original material for it to be unnecessary to rely on *double-entendre* for sales. The sexual metaphor of *King Spider Blues*, however, was highly inventive—certainly a cut above the average party blues.

> Let me be your king spider, I want to build my web on your wall. (x2)
> Then I want to catch your little flies, oooh, well, well, now, when they begin to fall.

> I'm a good web-builder, please let me build your web one time. (x2)
> Because, now, there ain't another spider, oooh, well, well, now, can build a web like mine.
>
> When I start to make my web, now, I goes round and around. (x2)
> But, now, when I get it almost finished, oooh, well, well (well, I draws) up and down.

Three days later Peetie was still in Chicago, but recording for Vocalion . He made *Hi-De-Ho Woman Blues* (rattlesnakes again), *Sorrow Hearted Blues*, *Up The Road Blues* and *Last Dime Blues*. On the last two, he chose to forgo his standard piano introduction, and instead used a more complex piano figure that unfortunately does not occur in any of his later records.

King of Spades and *Johnnie Blues* are both full of the self-confidence and arrogance that saw their fullest development in the three "stomps" several years later. In fact, *Johnnie Blues* was really the first stomp; it had the same fast tempo, the same attitude, but "Johnnie" was the subject of the song, not Peetie Wheatstraw. It was one of Peetie's best performances.

> The women all raving about Johnnie in this town. (x2)
> Now, he got something, oooh, well, well, make the women clown.
>
> He made them laugh and he made them cry. (x2)
> He have a sweet way of loving, oooh, well, well, and that's the reason why.
>
> He got something that will make them clown. (x2)
> Well, now, he made one woman jump overboard and drown.
>
> Don't never tell what the Johnnie man can do. (x2)
> Because that will make other women, oooh, well, well, want to clown over him, too.

Santa Claus Blues and *Lonesome Lonesome Blues* were made for Decca three months later. In the former song the usual Christmas worries and discomforts took on a new, potentially sexual, level of significance.

> Christmas almost here, what are you gonna do for me ? (x2)
> Am I gon' have a present, oooh, well, well, on your little Christmas tree ?
>
> I begin to worry when it is almost Christmas time. (x2)
> Now, you know, I wonder to myself, oooh, well, well, am I gonna be left behind?
>
> Eee, well, last Christmas, you made Santa Claus come to me. (x2)
> Now, you let me hang my stocking, oooh, well, well, on your little Christmas tree.
>
> If I don't get a present this Christmas, mama, I don't see the reason why. (x2)
> Because, now, you know, I don't never let, oooh, well, well, babe, Santa Claus pass you by.
>
> Now you's a evil-hearted woman, and, now, you got rocks in your jaws. (x2)
> And if you don't change your way, oooh, well, well, babe, I ain't gonna be your Santa Claus.

The second verse of *Lonesome Lonesome Blues* contained what must have been the most unusual request ever made of a "captain" in a song of the "I asked my captain..." type:

> Early one morning when they pull that lonesome chain. (x2)
> They says, "Boy, get ready, oooh, well, well, and answer to your name."
>
> Well, I asked my captain, could I use his phone. (x2)
> I want to call my baby, oooh, well, well, and tell her that I am gone.
>
> Goodbye, baby, well, I have gotta go. (x2)

But I won't be back, oooh, well, well, until nineteen and forty-four.

You could have needed me if you had wanted to. (x2)
Someday, now, you may need me, oooh, well, well, just as I did you.

Well, you was so deceitful, babe, I don't know why. (x2)
So your daddy's leaving, oooh, well, well, and I must say goodbye.

In the fourth verse above, Peetie tries to confront the mystique of romance with a jaundiced, practical eye when he exposes the voluntary aspects ("want") of a supposed involuntary feeling ("need").

One side of Decca 7170 was by Bumble Bee Slim (Amos Easton); the other side, *No Good Woman* (subtitled *Fighting Blues*), was labeled as by "Bumble Bee Slim and Peetie Wheatstraw" and was, in fact, a duet by them that is certainly worth quoting in full.

[spoken]
BB: Listen, Peetie, you been threatening me for four long years.
PW: So what?
BB: Uh, now listen; you know I love that woman, and you love her too. You's a man and I'm a man, and you've been talking all over town 'bout what you gonna do and everything.
PW: Well, now, what you gonna do about it?
BB: Well, you got to fight me now, Peetie.
PW: Well, boys, just don't fight; just play the blues, and sing a little while. Forget it.
BB: Forget it, huh?
PW: Yeah.
BB: Is that the way you feel?
[sung]
PW: Used to be my woman, I used to give her my last dime. (x2)
BB: [spoken] Are you telling me?
PW: During the bad depression, oooh, well, well, when change was hard to find.

BB: If that's your woman, you better pin her to your side. (x2)
If she ever flag my train, Lord knows I'm gonna let her ride.
PW: Well, now, we will call it square, that is strictly understood. (x2)
BB: [spoken] Call it square!
PW: After all of this noise, oooh, well, well, she don't mean one man no good.
BB: I"ve got a plenty women. Peetie, I don't need your funny kind. (x2)
PW: [spoken] Couldn't be funny.
BB: I would rather let you have her than to see you lose your mind.

By 1936 Peetie was definitely a well-established artist; he still recorded for Vocalion as well as Decca, but before the year was over, relations wlth Vocalion ceased and he became an exclusive Decca records artist. Before he left Vocalion, however, he made some of his best records. *First And Last Blues* and *True Blue Woman* were average, but *Kidnapper's Blues* was outstanding.

They kidnapped my baby, she was all I had. (x2)
They asked (her) for 10,000 ransom, oooh, well, well, you know, it made me feel so bad.

No kidnapper can do me this-a-way. (x2)
I'm going to the Chief Detective, oooh, well, well, and see what will he say.

I love my babe, and I want her to come on home. (x2)
But the low-down kidnapper, oooh, well, well, have taken my babe and gone.

I'd give them 10,000 dollars just to see her smiling face again. (x2)
She is all I got to live for, oooh, well, also she is my best friend.

The Chief Detective say, "I've got all my mens on the block. (x2)

And I'm telling everybody, oooh, well, well, this kidnapping must be stopped."

"Kidnappers Blues"
by PEETIE WHEATSTRAW
No 3249

3249 KIDNAPPERS BLUES and FROGGIE BLUES —Vocal, Piano, Guitar Acc. Peetie Wheatstraw 59c

Such imaginative constructions played a vital role in the blues—the impossibility of the situation made it intriguing. It was enjoyable to imagine that one might have $10,000 to give for the return of a ransomed loved one, just as it was pleasant to think that a missing Black woman would elicit so much attention from a Chief Detective. The song had humor, too, as well as a basis in reality. Even though it was extremely unlikely that a kidnapper with ransom in mind would target a lower-class black woman, there were other, less sophisticated sorts of abduction that occurred with some frequency in the black ghetto. And, of course, Peetie's imaginative composition also stimulated the imagination of his listeners. He even re-made the song for Decca six days later. From the same Vocalion session (13 February 1936), *Working Man* remained unissued. *Sweet Home Blues* and *Good Woman Blues* were coupled for release, and both sides were lyrically very good.

Here is *Sweet Home Blues*:

I was thinking about going home, I don't believe that I will go. (x2)

I'm going to stay away a long time, oooh, well, well, like I did once before.

My baby will be glad to see me come walking in her door. (x2)
Ahh, but now remember, oooh, well, she will never see me anymore.

Home is a happy place if you can make it that way. (x2)
Now, if you can't keep a happy home, oooh, well, well, will be the devil each and every day.

I try to be good every place I go. (x2)
But, now, you know, there will come a day, oooh, well, well, I will have some place I know.

Now, if I go home, do you think that is the best place to be? (x2)
Well, then again, if'n I go home, oooh, well, now, do you think she will be mean to me?

Good Woman Blues was one of the few songs Peetie made in which he awarded women unqualified praise, without regarding them as potential "mistreaters."

What makes me love my baby? She loved me when I was down. (x2)
Well, now, she was nice and kind, oooh, well, well, she did not dog me around.

You know, the most of the women, listen to what people say. (x2)
Well, but now, you know, my babe, oooh, well, well, she's just the other way.

Well, now, she give me money and kept me nice and clean (x2)
Well, now, you know, when I was down, oooh, well, my babe didn't treat me mean.

[spoken] Play it just a little bit, boy, and after I get through playing it, just beat it out a little.

Now I'm good to my baby since I'm up on my feet. (x2)
Well, now, I don't care, oooh, well, if I never see a woman on the street.

Peetie had a four-day recording session with Decca in New York commencing on 18 February 1936; on these sides, as on some later ones, the Georgia-born guitarist Kokomo Arnold accompanied him. Three months before Peetie made his first record, Kokomo was in Memphis recording for Victor; his first record, issued on Victor 23268 under the name "Gitfiddle Jim," was one of the Victor 23250-series items that is extremely scarce *and* exceptionally good. Unlike Peetie, Kokomo went unrecorded for the next four years. By 1936, however, he had been with Decca for two years, and his amazing agility with the slide guitar had made him one of their better selling country blues artists. Decca must have thought highly of Kokomo's popularity, because it issued all twelve songs from this session with his name on the label as accompanist, instead of just "Blues Singing with Piano and Guitar Accompaniment." On *Deep Sea Love* he was even listed erroneously as the pianist! The reverse of this record was *The First Shall Be Last And The Last Shall Be First*, which contained this powerful sexual image:

Well, the first woman I had, she made me get on my knees. (x2)
And had the nerve to ask me, oooh, well, well, if I liked limburger cheese.

Decca 7167 was unusual in other respects. Although there was nothing peculiar about the label for *The First Shall Be Last And The Last Shall Be First*, on *Deep Sea Love*, under Peetie's name, were the words "The High Sheriff from Hell." It was the only time that this sobriquet appeared on a record label.

Kokomo and Peetie worked well together, Kokomo's high, whining guitar notes providing electrifying, if occasionally off-key, contrast to Peetie's mellow piano. According to Henry Townsend, Peetie preferred to work without a guitarist,[7] and Kokomo indicated that he preferred working with Roosevelt Sykes or Joshua Altheimer.

To return to the other ten songs recorded at this session: *Working Man* was subtitled *Doin' The Best I Can*, and it was, indeed, another version of that song. One of Peetie's best-selling records, it was coupled with *Low Down Rascal*, which contained this interesting verse:

> If I catch you around my house, you better jump in some country well. (x2)
> Well, I'm gonna take my old shot-gun, oooh, well, well, and I'm gonna raise some country hell.

When I Get My Bonus was also sung to the melody of *Doin' The Best I Can* and it was coupled with *Coon Can Shorty*. The suggestive *Meat Cutter Blues* was coupled with Peetie's third song about the end of prohibition, *Old Good Whiskey Blues*:

> I have been drinking my good whiskey ever since it come back in. (x2)
> Now, now, I'm gonna drink my good whiskey, oooh, well, well, until it go out again.
>
> So please take my advice, and don't be no hooch-headed man. (x2)
> Ahh, because (they're) bootleggers over here, oooh, well, well, that poison every man they can.

Decca issued the remake of *Kidnapper's Blues* with *Poor Millionaire Blues*. In order to engage in optimistic and hopeful fantasy, one must transcend the frustrations of reality, and, as can be seen from some of the verses in *Poor Millionaire Blues*, Peetie was not always completely successful:

> Well, that's, that's all right, I will have a pay-day coming some old day. (x2)
> I just want you all to know, oooh, well, well, depression did not come to stay.
>
> Yes, I'm a poor boy today, tomorrow I may be a big millionaire. (x2)
> 'Cause I feel a break coming, oooh, well, well, uh, but I can't tell where.

In *Country Fool Blues*, Peetie referred to rattlesnakes for the fourth time. The symbol of the rattlesnake, with its phallic connotations, may have represented competition over women. On the reverse of the record was a detailed account of the effects of liquor, *Drinking Man Blues*.

> The jailer ask me, "Peetie, how come you so rough?" (x2)
> Well, now, I ain't bad, oooh, well, well, but I just been drinking that stuff.
>
> That stuff will kill you, but it just won't quit. (x2)
> It will get you to the place, oooh, well, well, that you don't care who you hit.

> I been drinking that stuff, and it went to my head. (x2)
> It made me hit the baby in the cradle, oooh, well, well, and kill my papa dead.
>
> It made me hit the policeman and knock him off his feet. (x2)
> Taken his pistol and his star, oooh, well, well, and walking up and down his beat.
>
> I been drinking that stuff, I been drinking it all my days. (x2)
> But the judge give me six months, oooh, well, well, to change my drinking ways.

Although one could consider Peetie's description a catalogue of the ill effects of liquor, he provided no statement of remorse. He stated simply, that he'd been drinking "all my days." Of course, Peetie and his listeners possibly drank, not in spite of the "bad" effects of whiskey, but because of them, the whiskey being useful as a stimulant and a relaxer of inhibitions, welcomed by those men and women who could find no socially condoned outlet for their frustrated desires.

Peetie's last session for Vocalion took place on 8–9 April. He was accompanied by an unknown guitarist (or guitarists), and lyrically and musically it was a high-quality session. His first song was *Jungle Man Blues*:

> I ain't nothing but a hobo, want somebody to help me carry my load. (x2)
> I have traveled the road so long, oooh, well, well, until it have made my shoulders sore.
>
> Well, now, I been in the jungle, three long nights and days. (x2)
> But I can't find no one, oooh, well, well, now, to help me on my way.
>
> Now one of these days, I won't be no jungle man. (x2)
> Well, now, I'll be to the place, oooh, well well, I won't have to go from hand to hand.

Vocalion

Not Licensed for Radio Broadcast (C 1348)

Vocal with Piano and Guitar Acc.

JUNGLE MAN BLUES
-Bunch-
PEETIE WHEATSTRAW
(The Devil's Son-In-Law)
03231

U.S. PAT. 1,637,544 BRUNSWICK RECORD CORPORATION

    The hobo jungle, or hoboville, was a fairly common sight during the depression when many people found themselves with neither jobs nor homes. In Chicago when hundreds of unemployed workers were already sleeping under the elevated train-tracks, a hoboville sprang up on Harrison and Canal Streets. It was an area the homeless used to provide some sort of shelter for themselves. Usually all they could obtain was a crude shack, constructed like a lean-to with scraps of newspaper and tar-paper for insulation. Life in these squalid conditions was horrid; the depression familiarized many people with a way of life previously known only to a wretched minority. One must remember that there were few people so impoverished that the depression failed to affect them, and the members of Peetie's social class were those who suffered the most. The truth-value of such songs as *Jungle Man Blues* is therefore quite high, for,

Hoboville at Harrison and Canal Streets, Chicago, 1932.

The poor and homeless found shelter wherever they could. This area later become an expressway.

whether Peetie himself spent few or many nights in a hobo jungle, the jungle itself was a stark reality to many members of the black lower class, the class by whom the blues were produced and for whom the blues existed.

The reverse of *Jungle Man Blues* was *Santa Fe Blues*, the only train blues Peetie recorded other than his various versions of *C And A Train Blues*.

> Ain't it a shame, ain't it a shame, it's a low-down dirty shame. (x2)
> My baby wrote for me, oooh, well, well, but the special agent won't let me ride this train.
>
> Goodbye, ol' Memphis, farewell to the state of Tennessee. (x2)
> Well, I'm going home to my baby, oooh, well, well, and she must come home to me.
>
> When you get lonesome, please sit down and write to me. (x2)
> If I don't come on the Great Northern, oooh, well, well, I'll be home on the Sante Fe.
>
> Well, now, goodbye, Memphis, oh, how I love you so. (x2)
> My babe has sent for me, oooh, well, well, and I swear I got to go.

Mistreated Love Blues was not very exciting, but its reverse was *Remember and Forget Blues*.

> It's so easy to remember and it's so hard to forget. (x2)
> The way my woman mistreats me, oooh, well, well, I ain't got over it yet.
>
> When I was working, people, she really had her sway. (x2)
> Because I gave her my money, oooh, well, well, and she lived in a great big way.
>
> She didn't have no worry, didn't hit a lick at a snake. (x2)
> She didn't even cook her meals, oooh, well, well, I mean she really had got a break.

Now I ain't got no money, no job can I find. (x2)
She tells me that she loves me, oooh, well, well, but she have changed her mind.

Now I ain't got nobody, I done put my love up on my shelf. (x2)
Since the woman I loved have deceived me, oooh, well, well, now, I don't want nobody else.

Apart from the last verse, this song, "oooh, well, well's" and all, was recorded twelve years later by the Texas bluesman Smokey Hogg, under the title *My Baby's Worrying Me* (Modern 20-615).

Don't Take A Chance was unremarkable, but the remaining titles all had excellent lyrics, at least in part. *Froggie Blues* was one.

I am watching these men that always grinning in my face. (x2)
They don't mean me no good, oooh, well, well, they just wants to take my place.

Now, if you feel froggie and want to hop my gal. (x2)
Now, don't be no fool, oooh, well, well, 'cause I take(n) you for my pal.

Let me tell you men how to keep your gal at home. (x2)
Just put her to bed, oooh, well, well, and roll her all night long.

You hug her and kiss her and squeeze her till she moans. (x2)
Then stop and hypnotize her, oooh, well well, and she sure won't leave home.

Block And Tackle contained one verse that certainly stimulated the imagination:

What she did to me, people, ain't never been done before. (x2)

Corrected to March 22, 1936
LOCAL TIME TABLES
Santa Fe
The
Atchison,
Topeka &
Santa Fe
AND
Panhandle & Santa Fe
Railway Companies

Vocalion
Not Licensed for Radio Broadcast
(C 1349)
Vocal with Piano and Guitar Acc.
SANTE FE BLUES
-Bunch-
PEETIE WHEATSTRAW
(The Devil's Son-In-Law)
03231
U.S. PAT. 1637544 BRUNSWICK RECORD CORPORATION

DECCA
(60539)
Vocal Blues, Piano Accompaniment by Kokomo Arnold
DEEP SEA LOVE
(WILLIAM BUNCH)
PEETIE WHEATSTRAW
(The High Sheriff from Hell)
7167 B

FULL-RANGE RECORDING
Vocalion
MADE IN U.S.A.-NOT LICENSED FOR RADIO BROADCAST
Vocal with
(C 1353)
Piano and Guitar Acc.
FROGGIE BLUES
-Harrison-
PEETIE WHEATSTRAW
(The Devil's Son-In-Law)
03249
U.S. PATENT 1637544 - LAB. COPY. 1937 BY BRUNSWICK RECORD CORPORATION

But she really made me like it, oooh, well, well, and I want to do it some more.

Cut Out Blues was the first of two versions of that song.

I'm gonna cut out my way of living, and I'm gonna change my ways. (x2)
Because I've got a funny feeling, oooh, well well, and I believe it will shorten my days.

I'm gonna cut out moaning and groaning about these no good dames. (x2)
Ahh, they don't care nothing about you, oooh, well, well, they just want your pay-day change.

I'm gon' cut out going to the station, gazing down the railroad track. (x2)
Because them double-crossing women left me, ooh, well, well, and won't come back.

I'm gon' cut out playing policy because my numbers just won't fall. (x2)
Somebody's put jinx on me, oooh, well, and I can't have no luck at all.

I'm gonna cut out all my troubles, start my life over again.(x2)
And when my (Toby) tells, oooh, well, I'm gonna cut in with some good (Jane).

I've always found the first line of the third verse particularly fascinating, included as it is in a list of the singer's "vices." "Going to the station, gazing down the railroad track," certainly the saddest vice of all!

Peetie ended his affiliation with Vocalion with a superior set of songs. He was to record for Decca for the rest of his life, but it was at the next four or five sessions that he produced what must be considered his best work.

" A Piano Player and a Rounder..."

Let us interrupt our discussion of Peetie's songs in order to see the impact he was having on the blues world. If we look at all the aspects of his influence, it is easy to see how tremendously important he was. Countless bluesmen imitated him; some sang his songs, some tried to sing in the same style, others even used his name.

Sometimes it is difficult to decide to which singer a song belonged. Of Peetie's *King Spider Blues*, for example, we can say that it may have influenced Johnny Shines, James DeBerry, and Muddy Waters, all of whom sang different versions of it, occasionally using Wheatstraw's intonations. But we don't know where Peetie found the song. Bessie Smith did a *Spider Man Blues*, and the composer credit on *King Spider Blues* is to her, so it may be that she influenced all three of the above singers and Peetie. Victoria Spivey also did an earlier *Spider Web Blues*. On the other hand, an artist as well-known as Peetie could be expected to play a large part in popularizing any song that he recorded, whether it was recorded earlier by someone else or not.

The lineages of other compositions are not so difficult to trace. I have already mentioned that John Henry Barbee recorded Peetie's *Six Weeks Old Blues* (though the composer credit on the later version is to Barbee), and we have also seen that Smokey Hogg recorded Peetie's *Remember And Forget Blues* as *My Baby's Worrying Me* (composer credit to Hogg). B. B. King recorded a *Mr Pawn Broker* (Crown CLP5188) that was remarkably similar to Peetie's *Pawn Broker Blues*, while the pianist Lazy Bill Lucas recorded Peetie's *Crazy With The Blues* (Wild 12M01) in 1969.

More numerous than those who sang Peetie's songs were those who tried to sing like him. Doubtless, even the now famous Robert Johnson was influenced by Peetie, at least to some extent, but there are plainer examples. Jack Dupree did a superb imitation of Peetie on his recording of *Rum Cola Blues* (Joe Davis 5100). Not only did Dupree use the "oooh, well, well" phrase, but he had even mastered the characteristic Wheatstraw inflections that occurred at the end of every verse Peetie sang.

I am not one who hears a strong Wheatstraw influence in every singer who used the "oooh, well, well" cry, but often more evidence than that exists. For example, singers like Casey Bill never inserted the "oooh, well, well" into their verses until after they had some contact with Peetie. In such cases, stylistic similarities can hardly be dismissed as coincidences. Besides Casey Bill, there was also Smokey Hogg. At his first recording session for Decca in 1937, Hogg was using Peetie's vocal style, and he continued to do so into the late '40s, as in *My Baby's Worrying Me* and *Suitcase Blues* (Modern 20-704). Then there was the obscure James Sherrill, who recorded as "Peanut the Kidnapper". *Silver Spade Blues* (ARC 7-09-65) sounded more like Peetie than any of the imitations mentioned so far. As Sherrill could sing in other styles, it is likely that his imitation of Peetie was intentional. Sherrill also record a *Suicide Blues*, but he did so several years *before* Peetie recorded his own version. Other singers whose vocal styles Peetie probably influenced include Shorty Bob Parker, Big Joe Williams, Johnny Shines, Georgia Slim and possibly Bukka White.

Of course, one cannot call every example of Peetie's influence imitation. The exchange of lyrics and styles that one finds in blues occurs in all other art forms, and it should in no way detract from an artist's reputation if his influences happen to be traceable. The stature of a unique artist like Jazz Gillum is hardly affected because he happened to use the "oooh, well, well" phrase consistently in one of his songs (*Deep Water Blues*, Bluebird 34-0709). Similarly one must judge the work of artists like Alec Seward and Louis Hayes on its own merits. Hayes's singing on their *Working Man Blues* (MGM 10770) sounds very much like Peetie's, but the performance is excellent, and would have been even if the vocal work had taken its inspiration from another source. But the performance did owe much to Peetie, and, though it does no discredit Hayes's originality, it interests us as another example of Peetie's wide-spread influence.

The clearest sign of Peetie's popularity than the fact that a number of singers used his name on their records in order to increase their own popularity. The East Coast bluesman Floyd "Dipper Boy" Council made at least one record that was labeled as by "The Devil's Daddy-in-Law." I have already mentioned how Jimmie Gordon was billed as "Peetie Wheatstraw's Brother," but if imitation is the sincerest form of flattery, then

Harmon Ray was Peetie's greatest admirer. He recorded with Big Joe [McCoy] and His Rhythm as "Peetie Wheatstraw's Buddy" and he recorded for Decca as Herman "Peetie Wheatstraw" Ray.

Ray was born in Indianapolis in 1914, but grew up in St Louis, hearing the records of Leroy Carr. He frequently saw Roosevelt Sykes and Walter Davis performing, and, we must assume, he heard the work of Peetie Wheatstraw whose style he took for his own. He began to work in the St Louis clubs and first met Peetie in 1935 at the Cabin Inn. When Peetie said, "Man, you sing just like me," Ray replied, "Man, *you* sing just like *me*."

Ray and Wheatstraw often worked together around the St Louis area, and sometimes traveled by car to the South to work. They often sang alternate verses as a crowd pleaser, and while Ray accompanied Wheatstraw to Chicago for the latter's recording sessions, they never recorded together.

This man has been tentatively identified as Harmon Ray, "Peetie Wheatstraw's Buddy."

Ray made his recording debut less than two months after Peetie died, no doubt thanks to Lester Melrose who suggested he appear as "Peetie Wheatstraw's Buddy."[8] The first picture that circulated with the reputation of being a photograph of Peetie seems in fact to have been of Harmon Ray.

Robert Lee McCoy was a harmonica player as well as a highly skilled slide guitarist, and he played the former instrument on at least one of Peetie's recording sessions. About the same time, he recorded for Decca himself, and his records were labelled as by "Peetie's Boy." They in no way resemble Wheatstraw performances, and it is possible that someone at Decca, rather than McCoy himself, decided to put "Peetie's Boy" on them. Henry Townsend remembered that "Robert Lee McCoy was a lone wolf. He played with Peetie a few times, just like he played with everybody a few times. But I wouldn't call him a good friend of Peetie's! No, he was a loner, one of those type guys..."

A picture of Charlie Jordan that had been signed "The Devil's Son-in-Law" has circulated for years. Because of the signature, many people thought the picture was of Peetie, at least until an authentic photograph began to circulate. It is not known if Jordan himself wrote the legend on the picture, but whoever did so probably had publicity for Jordan in mind.

A year after the first printing of this work, *Superfly* hit the movie screen, and five years later in 1977 Rudy Ray Moore starred in *Petey Wheatstraw, the Devil's Son-in-Law*, wherein Moore played a distinctly Superfly-inspired character.

Certainly the most unusual appearance of the name Peetie Wheatstraw occurs in Ralph Ellison's novel *Invisible Man*. In the story, the narrator is wandering through the streets of Harlem when he encounters a blues-singing black man pushing a cart full of discarded blueprints. The cart-man is a jive-talker of high caliber, and his fast spoken phrases are too much for the younger man to understand. In a half-candid moment of greater clarity, the cart pusher reveals himself as "Peter Wheatstraw ... the Devil's only son-in- law... a piano player and a rounder, a whiskey drinker and a pavement pounder." There could not have been a more enticing description, and one could only wonder at the exact nature of the inspiration for Ellison's character.

Ellison's own comments have been ambiguous. Leroy Pierson, who has spent a considerable amount of time researching the St Louis blues singers, managed to secure a short interview with Ellison, and he found that the author had not only known Peetie but played trumpet with him occasionally in the bars of St Louis. According to Ellison, the character in the novel was inspired by Peetie's general personality and patterns of speech. The other attributes of the cart-pusher were entirely fictional. Thus was summed up Ellison's relationship to Wheatstraw in the first (1971) edition of this book.

But on 11 March, 1988, Ellison answered Robert G. O'Meally's query about "his use of the folk character Peter Wheatstraw" with these words, which O'Meally published in the *Atlantic Monthly* in his review of Ellison's just-released novel, *Juneteenth*:

"As far as *I* know 'Peter Wheatstraw' was not, and is not, a living individual, but a character born of Afro-American mythology. Unfortunately, I know nothing of his legend, nor of how it originated, but as a boy who had friends who were aspiring pool & billiards sharks I was familiar with 'Peter Wheatstraw' as one half of a dual persona that was evoked in the form of a frontier brag (or boast) when players wished to challenge prospective opponents to combat upon the green cloth of pool tables. The name of Wheatstraw's other half (by the way, he was never 'Peetie' but always 'Peter') was 'Lord God Stingerroy.'

"Thus when a challenger banged through the swinging doors of the pool parlor he'd stamp his foot and let out a belligerent roar that went: My name is Peter Wheatstraw I'm the Devil's only son-in-law — So who wants to play [or shoot] the Devil's Son — Lord God Stingerroy!

"That is the extent of my Wheatstraw knowledge, and the circumstance out of which I appropriated the name when I used it in my novel. In other words, I 'novelized' it, and you'll note that it appears at a point when the narrator is being challenged to draw upon his folk-based background for orientation and survival.... For a novelist and descendant of storytellers, such items of folk tradition are part of his inheritance and are to be used—much as the composers of music used the folk music of their individual backgrounds—in the expression of his own unique vision. They are part of the mother lode which supports his storytelling and are as free to be used by the conscious writer as they are by the oral tellers of tales." [9]

No doubt the truth lies between both of Ellison's earlier and later statements—the blues singer as well as the hero of the toast inspired the character in the novel—but we can more fully understand the unique appearance of Peetie Wheatstraw in the *Invisible Man* if we take a closer look at Ellison's own history and development.

While modern commentators often emphasize Ellison's relative conservatism, or at least his anti-leftism, he spent the late 1930s and early 1940s hewing to the line of the Communist Party of the United States (CPUSA), and writing for such leftist periodicals as *New Masses, Direction*, and *New Challenge*. Ellison's disillusionment with the Communist left seemed to come from the CPUSA's giving short shrift to segregation and other African American concerns in favorite of the war effort. He also was disappointed with the lack of sophistication in the American left and its refusal to merge Freud and Marx as a way of confronting the irrational, which in the US took the form of anti-Black prejudice and discrimination among whites.[10]

Barbara Foley has drawn our attention to the fact that as early as 1939 Ellison perceived the links between vernacular speech and proletarian politics, just as he saw folklore as a site of resistance, an important consideration when assessing the appearance of Peetie Wheatstraw in Ellison's work! But for Ellison c. 1939, the transcendence of the rural migrant folk into the self-conscious, class conscious, urban trade unionist was more significant.[11] Ellison's fondness for blues is genuine and understanding, but like his friend Albert Murray, he felt that it was the tranformation of blues into "more precise vocabularies" that deserved the most attention.

He even took William Attaway to task for the way the characters in his novel, *Let Me Breathe Thunder*, failed to undergo a thorough evolution in class consciousness. While he could deftly delineate the adventures of the proletarian character, Attaway couldn't *imagine* his evolution into a class conscious unionist. And yet Ellison's own conception of Peter Wheatstraw, a dozen years later, attributes tremendous power to the Wheatstraw character, a power that the cartman cannot transmit and hero cannot absorb.

Houston Baker criticizes Ellison for this parallel failure: "Which is not to say there are no rebellious hipsters, hustling cartmen named Wheatstraw, and bodacious chameleon

Rhineharts in Ellison's northern imaginary. No, it is not that Ellison missed the futuristic black 'underground' altogether. He simply failed, or refused, to inscribe the process of that 'underground' transforming itself into a field of revolutionary energy that changed the ways of black American folk for all time." When Blacks were transforming morality, equality and reponsibility from affirmitive notions into affirmitive actions, Ellison was fairly silent, Baker points out, and he theorizes that Ellison was cowed by the overwhelming tide of McCarthyism. Whatever the reason, Ellison would not lend his prestige to the cause of Black Liberation. [12]

Given all these foundations and contradictions, we immediately sense what a complex character was the Peter Wheatstraw who made his appearance in a few pages of *Invisible Man*. Was he a blues singer, the personification of the blues itself, a paradigmatic proletarian, an evocation of downhome, rural and folk values, or, as I believe and others have argued, a combination of all of these? Our hero, you will recall, before Wheatstraw makes his appearance at the beginning of Chapter 9, has just been given his walking papers from the university for an act of monumental indiscretion. He holds in his pocket a highly valued letter of recommendation, not realizing that the letter instructs the reader to give the bearer no assistance and is actually a letter of denunciation.

Trying desperately to snatch victory from the jaws of defeat, he has every reason to be terribly depressed, but he is buoying himself up with the thought of what success will be his, thanks to his letter of recommendation! This is his situation when he meets the jive talking cart-pusher, carrying a load of discarded blueprints, singing the blues, calling himself Peter Wheatstraw, the Devil's Son-in-Law. Wheatstraw confronts our hero with Black English references that he finds nearly opaque—"Is you got the *dog*?"—and after Wheatstraw castigates him with, "Now I know you from down home...," he feels embarrassed, angry, and uncomfortable. The subject changes from dogs to bears, and the protagonist is moved to remember down home sayings about Jack the Rabbit and Jack the Bear, but he can't recall their wording or their meaning. They were "long forgotten but brought a wave of homesickness" and he felt "a certain comfort" walking along next to the cart-pusher.

To emphasize the hero's ambivalence at this point may seem trite, but we can't help but wonder at its cause and its origin. For he obviously is drawn to this essence-of-the-folk character, just as he is repelled by him and beckoned forward by his conception of his own seriousness of purpose. The discarded blueprints represent, according to their current owner, the changed plans of white folks. "Folks is always making plans and changing them," he says, eerily echoing the protagonist's fate. When the hero notes that it's important to stick to one's plan, Wheatstraw suddenly stops and addresses him gravely, "You kinda young, daddy-o," without ever explaining his words or his abrupt turn to seriousness.

Wheatstraw's uncanny ability to see into the thoughts and actions of the hero hints at the significance Ellison assigns him. The bearer of the folk heritage of an entire race, Wheatstraw embodies a multiplicity of virtues that Ellison only dimly sketched, as if to hint at the distance the hero has placed between himself and these values through his sophistication and alienation. Wheatstraw's words are few. The amount of wisdom he attempts to transmit in these few words is vast, but this is too much for the hero who is learning his lessons the hard way.

Langston Hughes created a similar character in his stories about Simple (which began to appear in 1945 and may have inspired Ellison), and Walter Mosely has created a similar figure recently in his Tempest Tales for *Savoy* magazine. Simple is the personification of everyman, the folk tradition, the Black Experience at large (and small). His simple arguments with his more sophisticated interlocuter always carry far more weight than their form would suggest, and they are always persuasive in spite of their crudity and simplicity.

The Wheatstraw episode ends with the cart-pusher heading down hill, singing "She's got feet like a monkey, legs like a mad bulldog," and the hero trying desperately to discern the meaning of the lyrics through a literal analysis: "...no woman fitted that description.... Was it a sphinx?" Did he love her or hate her? How could anyone love him? Or her, if she fit that description? The hero gives up on it, for "in order to travel far, you had to be detached." He has given up a chance at redemption, through his heritage, his roots—although he isn't conscious of it—in hopes of redemption through a more literal process of pursuit of bourgeois success. And in his attempt to understand a blues song about a woman, he has reminded us that in our pursuit of knowledge, facts are useless where poetic facts are called for.

Ellison's Peter Wheatstraw character refuses to reveal its sharpest edges, but is our own Peetie Wheatstraw, drawn from life instead of fiction, any less elusive? Twice I've come across persons bearing the name Peetie Wheatstraw, and in at least the first instance, the blues singer was undoubtedly the source of inspiration. The first case occurred in Louisville, Kentucky, in the '60s, nearly twenty years after Peetie died. I was looking through a pile of records in the home of an elderly black woman, and I found Peetie's *Crazy With The Blues.* When I mentioned that he was one of my favorite artists, she replied that not only had she always liked his records, but she had the pleasure of meeting him in Tennessee several weeks before. She was unmoved by my disbelief, and, although she could supply no more information about him, she insisted that it was *the* Peetie Wheatstraw that she had just met.

Only a short time later I encountered the second Peetie Wheatstraw of the year. A short, light-skinned man, looking nothing like Peetie, came into the Louisville record shop where I worked. He was snapping his fingers and jumping up and down excitedly; he began to shout, "I'm Peetie Wheatstraw, the Devil's Son-in-Law, that's who I am, Peetie Wheatstraw from Alabam'."

Charlie Jordan labeled "Devil's Son-in-Law.

"We Used to Have Luck in the Valley..."

By the end of 1936 Peetie was performing magnificently. The first of his excellent Decca sessions was held on 26 October, and a string bass and Kokomo Arnold accompanied him on all but the first two songs; for these he was joined by an unknown guitarist. *When A Man Gets Down* was a bitter reflection on the hypocrisy of friends and acquaintances:

> When a man is down, feel like he ain't got no friends at all. (x2)
> It seem like everybody, want to knock him around like he's an old ball.
>
> When it comes to women, he can't have no luck at all. (x2)
> They want to put a halter on him, oooh, well, and tie him up like a mule in a stall.
>
> When he go around his used-to-be woman, one he has give a real good time. (x2)
> Then again, you know, if he ask her for her salary, if she got a dollar, she will swear that she ain't got a dime.
>
> When he walks in to see his old gang with whom he used to drink. (x2)
> Well, then, if he asks them for a little taste, oooh, well, they say, "Oh, that's just what you think."
>
> Now, men, when you are down, one thing you must do. (x2)
> When you get (up), try to remember everybody that mistreated you.

I Don't Want No Pretty Faced Woman began in a hopeful vein, but it too ended with bitterness, or at least resignation.

> No pretty faces for me, I have seen them all my life. (x2)
> What I want is some good woman, oooh, well, well, who'll make me a sweet little wife.

> No paint and powder for me, no bobbed hair and (shaved-up?) head. (x2)
> Now, they don't even know, oooh, well, how much salt to put in your bread.
>
> I don't want no jazz-baby, they ain't even on my mind. (x2)
> I know I wouldn't get a chance with her, oooh, well, because some other man would have her all the time.
>
> I don't want no hooch-drinker, they just makes me sick. (x2)
> They'll play like they're in their whiskey, oooh, well, just to do you a low-down dirty trick.
>
> Ah, so I don't believe I'll marry, don't believe I'll settle down. (x2)
> I'm gonna catch the first train out, oooh, well, well, and leave this bad luck town.

To Peetie, a good woman was indeed hard to find. There are countless references to "no good women" and the like in his blues, and his arrogant self-confidence was a response to the reality that he found unpleasant.

The theme was continued in *False Hearted Woman*, the fourth verse of which contained a remarkable curse:

> I'm here in prison longing to be free. (x2)
> A false hearted woman, oooh, well, well, is the downfall of me.
>
> She caused me to steal all a working man could save. (x2)
> Ahh, she nearly caused for me, oooh, well, well, to be in my grave.
>
> She turn her back on me, time I landed in jail. (x2)
> Ah, well, she wouldn't even write, oooh, well, well, send poor me no mail.
>
> May bad luck overtake you, pile up on you in a heap. (x2)
> Well, you are nothing but a crook, may around you, now, you know, death may creep.

Now I have got to be old, and just about turning gray. (x2)
No other false hearted woman, oooh, well, well, can drive me thisaway.

Little House, subtitled *I'm Gonna Chase These Peppers*, was a rhythmic, unusually swinging blues, and its first verses contained highly original material.

Little house over yonder with the doors all painted green. (x2)
That's my woman's house near the corner, oooh, well, well, where you don't see no screen.

My cat is got the measles, dog has got the whooping cough. (x2)
You might as well (to be easy), woman, oooh, well, because I'm gonna be your boss.

Now, I ain't gonna marry, and I ain't gonna settle down. (x2)
I'm gonna stay right here, oooh, well, well, and run these peppers down.

I am going to Chicago to get my hambone boiled. (x2)
Because these St Louis women, oooh, well, going to let my hambone spoil.

Beggar Man Blues was coupled with the biblical-sounding *Fairasee Woman* (subtitled *Memphis Woman*):

My baby swears she don't love nobody but me. (x2)
So I'm gonna take her, oooh, well, and make her my fairasee.

One time she mistreated me, she treated me worser than a dirty dog. (x2)
But I had a pocketful of dollars, oooh, well, and she saw that I wasn't on the hog.

Now, we both is broke and can't hardly scout. (x2)

Now, we ain't got a dime, oooh, well, and the landlord's gonna put us out.

When you go to Memphis, you should stop by Church's land.
When you go to Memphis, you should stop by Church's hall.
And watch the fairasee women, oooh, well, well, cock it on the wall.

Now my woman is from Memphis, and she sure is good to me. (x2)
So I'm gonna keep her, oooh, well, and make her my fairasee.

One of the things that made *Fairasee Woman* extraordinary was the number of unusual terms it contained. Besides the enigmatic "(Church's) hall" is the title of the song itself. None of the singers I spoke to had heard the term "fairasee" (a misspelling of Pharisee?) used in this way, and unless it simply referred to women from Memphis, as the subtitle seems to suggest, its true meaning remains hidden. The use of the word "scout" in a blues song is also quite rare. Rather more common was "on the hog," which was used at least once on record by the Georgia artist Peg Leg Howell. The phrase means "broke," "down and out," and it was familiar to Odum and Johnson who mentioned it in their 1926 study *The Negro And His Songs*. A verse quite similar to "cock it on the wall" was recorded by Louise Johnson in 1930 in a song titled *On The Wall* (Paramount 13008).

At his next session, on 26 March 1937, Peetie was accompanied by an unknown guitar and bass, and he opened with the fascinating *Crazy With The Blues*.

I wake up this morning, just crazy with the blues. (x2)
I can't even tell, oooh, well, well, the difference in my shoes.

I'm just a crazy fool, I can't do a thing. (x2)
I'm just jumping around here, oooh, well, well, now, like a monkey on the end of a string.

> I went downtown this morning with my hat on upside down. (x2)
> The people looked at me like they thought that I was a country clown.
>
> I heard somebody call me, it was the policeman on his beat. (x2)
> Well, well, now, he just wanted to tell me, oooh, well, well, that I was driving on the wrong side of the street.
>
> Folks, I keep on telling you that I'm just a-crazy with the blues. (x2)
> I'm going to the railroad, then to the river, oooh, well, well, but I don't know which one that I will choose.

Other songs from this session included *Ramblin' Man*, in which Peetie referred to himself as "Ramblin' Sam," and *Would You Would You Mama*, a better than average performance which featured smoothly rolling piano and a compelling delivery.

> Now, would you, would you, mama, stop your messin' ways?
> Now, would you, would you, mama, stop and play on your horn?
> Would you, now, would you, mama, oooh, well, well, stop causing me to grieve and moan?

Crapshooter's Blues was also more interesting than the typical gambling blues, the gambler in this case being Peetie's woman.

> My baby's a crapshooter, and she shoots 'em like a man. (x2)
> And ever since she's being shooting crap, oooh, well, well, she's been going from hand to hand.
>
> Sometime she win, but the most time she lose. (x2)
> Boys, now, when she lose, oooh, well, well, then I have the crapshootin' blues.
>
> She told me to always bet that the dice won't pass. (x2)

> But every time since I been betting that way, oooh, well, well, I've been having a raggedy yas, yas, yas.
>
> I am telling all you crapshooters, now to let crapshooting go. (x2)
> 'Cause, now, you will be stone bare-footed, oooh, well, well, then again and out of dough.

But the most significant and important songs Peetie recorded that day were *Peetie Wheatstraw Stomp* and *Peetie Wheatstraw Stomp No. 2*. Here is the first:

> Women all raving about Peetie Wheatstraw in this land. (x2)
> He got some of these women, now, going from hand to hand.
>
> Don't tell all the girls what that Peetie Wheatstraw do. (x2)
> That will cause suspicion, now, you know, they will try him, too.
>
> [spoken] Now play a little bit, boy, let's see how it sounds.
>
> If you want to see the women and men clown. (x2)
> Just let that Peetie Wheatstraw come into your town.
>
> I am Peetie Wheatstraw, the High Sheriff from Hell. (x2)
> The way I strut my stuff, oooh, well, now, you never can tell.
>
> [spoken] Now do your stuff, Peetie.

and the second:

> Everybody hollering, "Here come that Peetie Wheatstraw." (x2)
> "Now, he's better known by the Devil's Son-in-Law."
>
> Everybody wondering what the Peetie Wheatstraw do. (x2)
> 'Cause every time you hear him, he's coming out with something new.

[spoken] Show 'em what Peetie Wheatstraw do, boy.

He makes some happy, some he make cry. (x2)
Well, now, he made one old lady go hang herself and die.

This is Peetie Wheatstraw, I'm always on the line. (x2)
Save up your nickels and dimes, you can come up and see
   me some time.
[spoken] Play it a little bit, boy.... Now good folks, do what
   I say. If you got it, spend it. Save your nickels and dimes,
   you can come up and see me some time.

    Boisterous, self-assured, refusing the slightest commitment to humility; these are the attributes of the character who emerges

The Tennessee guitarist and mandolinist James "Yank" Rachell, who recorded with Sleepy John Estes and Sonny Boy Williamson. Rachell knew Peetie in St Louis in 1940.

from the "stomps." The reconstruction of a personality for a singer whose death occurred years ago is no easy task, but we do have a few clues. In addition to the irrevocable and lyrically commanding outline that has started to take shape, we have the testimony of others who were alive during Peetie's time.

"Known to 'jive' fans as 'Peetie Wheatstraw'" said the *East St Louis Metro-Journal*, in its article describing the collision that killed Peetie. Henry Townsend agreed: "I would say that Peetie's personality was very similar to the one on the records [the "stomps"]. He was that kind of person. You know, a jive-type person." According to Honeyboy Edwards, Peetie lived with a white woman and owned a little white dog. "He was a big shot down there, got dressed up every day and walked that dog down the street on a little chain."[13]

Then we have the portrait Ralph Ellison drew so evocatively in his novel. Yank Rachell, the Tennessee bluesman who spent a few years in St Louis, also knew Peetie. "Sure, I remember Peetie Wheatstraw—the Devil's Son-in-Law—he had a long head. He liked his liquor, but I never heard nothing bad about Peetie Wheatstraw. He had what you call a nice personality, easy to get along with."

Even with such testimony, our picture is far from complete. Considering the lyrics of the "stomps," we may first need to determine how much of the material is factual. If we consider the "stomps" fantasy, Peetie very probably lived this fantasy as well as sang about it, if Townsend's testimony is accurate. But then, the separation of fantasy from reality is not always necessary for our purposes. We can see that this is so if we investigate Peetie's attitude towards women, for example, using the lyrics as our guide. We can say that however Peetie actually treated women, his songs tell us how he *felt* about them. There are some who would point out the male supremacist content of the lyrics and dismiss it at that, but what is needed here is an analysis, not a dismissal. Male chauvinism has always been rampant in the blues, and these issues are just beginning to be addressed analytically.[14]

We find, then, that our picture of Peetie only occasionally appears in sharp focus, remaining, for the rest of the time, vague and obscure. More is to be done, if we are to piece together the available fragments of the story of the Devil's Son-in-Law. Fortunately, Peetie left us many more songs to discuss. Through them we may expect to gain much insight into the atmosphere that surrounded Peetie in East St Louis during the last years of his life. Through them, too, we may be able to isolate a few of those facts that might make our picture of Peetie Wheatstraw somewhat richer in detail.

Four days after recording *Peetie Wheatstraw Stomp* and *Peetie Wheatstraw Stomp No.2,* Peetie was back at the Chicago studio. With him for the last time was Kokomo Arnold, and they recorded only two songs, *Give Me Black Or Brown,* and *Working On The Project*:

> I was working on the project, begging the relief for shoes. (x2)
> Because the rock and concrete, oooh, well, well, they's giving my feet the blues.
>
> Working on the project with holes all in my clothes. (x2)
> Trying to make me a dime, oooh, well, well, to keep the rent man from putting me outdoors.
>
> I am working on the project trying to make both ends meet. (x2)
> But the payday is so long, oooh, well, well, until the grocery man won't let me eat.
>
> Working on the project, my gal's spending all my dough. (x2)
> Now, I have waked up on her, oooh, well, well, and I won't be that weak no more.
>
> Working on the project with payday three or four weeks away. (x2)
> Now, how can you make (ends) meet, oooh, well, well, well, when you can't get no pay?

Seven months later, accompanied by an unknown guitar and bass, he made *New Working On The Project*:

> Working on the project, what a scared man, you know. (x2)
> Because every time I look around, oooh, well, well, somebody's getting their 304.

WPA workers at the St Louis riverfront. When this photo appeared in the *St Louis Post-Dispatch* of 25 February 1936, it bore the caption "1400 WPA Men Enjoy Spring Day on Levee."

WPA laborers back at work, 31 October 1939, following a strike over unhealthy conditions on the job. After the strike they were given hip boots.

Working on the project with a big furniture bill to pay. (x2)
But time I got my 304, oooh, well, well, the furniture man come and taken my furniture away.

Working on the project, the rent man is knocking on my door. (x2)
I'm sorry, Mr Rent Man, oooh, well, well, I just got my 304.

Working on the project, my pardner got his 304, too. (x2)
So you better look out, oooh, well, well, 'cause tomorrow it may be you.

Working on the project, a 304 may make you cry. (x2)
There's one thing sure, you can tell the project goodbye.

The Works Progress Administration (later called the Work Projects Administration) was a Federal relief program which operated from 1935 until 1939. Begun after the cessation of the CWA and the FERA, the WPA provided jobs for all sorts of laborers, as well as writers and artists. Eighty per cent of the WPA jobs, however, were in construction work, and as might be expected, many blues singers sang about the Project. Casey Bill even made an anti-WPA blues. While most people agree that in those days one was lucky to have any job, WPA or not, the black worker was still confronted with a number of difficulties, many of them sadly familiar. Also, the newspapers were full of stories like "Many Idle While Waiting for $591,000 Relief Job to Get Under Way." When there were jobs, the pay was quite low, though the Project did pay slightly more than a number of other jobs that were available to blacks. Whatever the amount, a WPA payroll could mean the difference between a small meal or no meal at all, and the workers dreaded the appearance of a 304 slip in their pay envelope, for a 304 meant they were no longer needed. Peetie made *304 Blues* at his next recording session, and life "on the project" was painted in less oppressive colors.

I was working on the project three or four months ago. (x2)
Since I ha' got my 304, oooh, well, well, my baby don't want me no more.

When I was working on the project, I had everything I need. (x2)
But since I got my 304, oooh, well, well, I can't even get a feed.

When I was working on the project, women was no object to me. (x2)
But since I got my 304, oooh, well, well, not a one of them can I see.

When I was working on the project, I drink my good whiskey, beer and wine. (x2)
But since I got my 304, oooh, well, these drinks is hard to find.

Goodbye, everybody, this is all I have to say. (x2)
But since I got my 304, oooh, well, well, my good woman, she have gone astray.

On the session at which he recorded *New Working On The Project*, Peetie also recorded the rather dull *Baby Lou, Baby Lou* and *Sick Bed Blues*. Other songs recorded that day included *Devilment Blues* and *I'm Gonna Cut Out Everything*, the latter being the second version of *Cut Out Blues*. The most interesting song of the day, and probably one of the most interesting Peetie ever made, was *Third Street's Going Down*.

We used to have luck in the "Valley," but the girls had to move way out of town. (x2)
Some moved in the alley, oooh, well, well, because Third Street is going down.

I had a girl on St Louis Avenue, but Third Street she hung around. (x2)
But the law got so hot, oooh, well, well, until Third Street is going down.

I waked up one morning, my face all full of frowns. (x2)
Ahh I [heard] nothing but my baby, "Ooooh, well, well, brown, Third Street is going down."

DECCA

TRADE MARK REGISTERED

NOT LICENSED FOR RADIO BROADCAST

(91324)

Blues Singing with Piano, Bass and Guitar

THIRD STREET'S GOING DOWN
(Jordan)

PEETIE WHEATSTRAW
(The Devil's Son-In-Law)

7379 B

MANUFACTURED IN U.S.A. BY DECCA RECORDS, INC.

[spoken] Play it, lemme hear it, now—you don't know how we sound.

The city hired Mr Keeler to put a highway through that part of town. (x2)
And the law told the girls to move, oooh, well, well,
"'cause we're tearing Third Street down."

Third Street ran through the heart of the East St Louis district known as the "Valley," an extremely tough area full of brothels, gambling houses, saloons and the like. Peetie's house was in the north end of the district at 468a North Third Street, just south of Ohio Street. Not only was East St Louis's red light district being torn down; it was Peetie's house, too. St Louis Avenue, also

St Louis Street scene, 1970.

Lonnie Johnson, c. 1928,
ten years before he
recorded with Peetie.

mentioned in the song, intersected Third Street two blocks south of Ohio Street; it, too, was slated for destruction. The bourgeois black citizenry of East St Louis looked down upon the residents of the "Valley", but to Peetie and and many others the "Valley" was home, and in the many clubs and bars of the district, the blues flourished.

It would be impossible to count the number of times the district was "closed," only to reopen within a few days or weeks. As well as being subjected to numerous temporary interferences, engendered by election promises and pseudo-reform campaigns, the "Valley" was the target of various urban renewal programs. One of these programs was the subject of *Third Street's Going Down*, but since these projects were slow to begin, even when scheduled, it is difficult to tell exactly which one inspired Peetie's song. A *St Louis Post-Dispatch* photograph taken more than ten years later, in 1948, shows one such operation beginning at an intersection, probably that at Third Street and St Louis Avenue.

Today virtually nothing is left of Third Street or the "Valley." South Third Street is surrounded by fields of sunflowers, while North Third Street, where Peetie lived, is an expressway bordered by a railroad yard. The public institutions which can usually be expected to house documents of historic interest have surprisingly little on the "Valley," but one can fine an excellent description of life in that district, as well as a discussion of the East St Louis political machine that enabled the "Valley" to flourish, in Elliott Rudwick's *Race Riot In East St Louis, July 2,1917.*

For his next session, on 1 April 1938, Peetie teamed up with the virtuoso guitarist Lonnie Johnson. Lonnie, who was born in New Orleans, had spent a number of years in St Louis, where he was quite well known, and by the time he recorded with Peetie he was one of the most popular blues recording artists in the country. He had made scores of records under his own name, and had accompanied numerous blues singers, from Victoria Spivey to Texas Alexander. He had also recorded some guitar duets with the white guitarist Eddie Lang, which, with his solos on several Louis Armstrong and Duke Ellington recordings, represent some of the finest guitar work ever produced in the 1920s. Lonnie's records with Peetie were probably no challenge to him, and it must be admitted that they certainly were not his

One of the few surviving photographs of the "Valley."
The view is towards the downtown area (east), from Second or Third Street.

Third Street and the "Valley," 1970.

best work. Still, the most typical accompaniments were more than adequate, and the change in sidemen was unfortunately necessary to keep Peetie's records from becoming musically monotonous. We will see that, within a few years, all efforts in this direction failed utterly, and little was left to Peetie's records but the lyrics.

Peetie and Lonnie recorded *304 Blues* and ten other songs. These included the suggestive *Banana Man*, the somewhat humorous *The Wrong Woman*, on which Lonnie was at his worst, and *Hard Headed Black Gal*. Also recorded were the dull and uninventive *Saturday Night Blues* and *Good Little Thing*, but *Road Tramp Blues* was an excellent example of a hobo song:

> I have walked this lonesome road till my feet is too sore to walk. (x2)
> I begged scraps from the people, oooh, well, well, till my tongue is too stiff to talk.
>
> I'm going to tell you women something that I really ain't gonna do. (x2)
> That I give you women (my labor? my loving?) oooh, well, well, and my money, too.
>
> Anybody can tell you people that I ain't no lazy man. (x2)
> But I guess I'll have to go to the poor house, oooh, well, brown, and do the best I can.
>
> I am what I am and all I was born to be. (x2)
> Now hard luck is in my family, oooh, well, well, and it's rolling down on me.
>
> When I get over my troubles, I'm gonna bring my money down. (x2)
> And change my way of living, oooh, well, well, so I won't have to tramp around.

What More Can A Man Do was a 16-bar blues that featured some brilliant guitar work, while *Sweet Lucille* contained a number of uncommon images:

> Boys, I got a girl, and her name is Miss Lucille. (x2)
> Then again, the way that she love, oooh, well, well, will make your head spin like a wheel.
>
> She have got three gold teeth, and she got two gold crowns. (x2)
> Boys, I'm here to tell you, oooh, well, well, she ain't no hand me down.
>
> If anybody should ask you about sweet Lucille. (x2)
> Please tell them that's my gal, oooh, well, then again, and she is my steering wheel.

On the reverse of *Sweet Lucille* was *Cake Alley*:

> There's a place in St Louis, they call Cake Alley, you know. (x2)
> It is a very tough place, oooh, well, well, where all the bums do love to go.
>
> Cake Alley runs from Blair Avenue on out to Fifteenth Street. (x2)
> But the good things you can get in Cake Alley, oooh, well, well, I swear it can't be beat.
>
> When you go in Cake Alley, you better know just what to do. (x2)
> Because, now, the bums in Cake Alley, oooh, well, well, will take your money from you.
>
> I was living in Cake Alley a very short time ago. (x2)
> But that's where I left my sweet woman, oooh, well, well, and I don't go there no more.
>
> The reason they call it Cake Alley, because the cakes is very (sweet). (x2)
> And like the bums in Cake Alley, oooh, well, well, they knock you off your feet.

The lyrics of *Cake Alley* obviously called for some field work, so on one of my trips to St Louis I drove out to Fifteenth

Street, just north of Biddle Street. This was the southern-most tip of St Louis's largest black ghetto, not far from the Biddle Street bars which formerly featured Peetie, Darby, Townsend, and the other St Louis bluesmen; it was also only a few blocks from "Deep Morgan." Henry Brown had recorded a blues about "Deep Morgan," and Henry Spaulding a *Biddle Street Blues*. It was left to Peetie to commemorate the block-long Cake Alley.

Cake Alley as it was in 1970.

Although Blair Avenue was on the map, we could find no trace of it. We did find two Fourteenth Streets, running parallel a block apart, and we soon discovered that the western one was formerly called Blair Avenue. In the short four-block area where Blair and Fifteenth ran parallel, there were three alleys. On questioning the local residents to find out which alley was the Cake Alley, the mystery soon dissolved. On the corner of Blair Avenue and the southernmost alley there had stood, at one time, a bakery, or, as one resident called it, a "cake place." This was Cake Alley, though there certainly wasn't much left of it now. None of the people spoken to had lived there long enough (more than thirty years) to remember how infamous it may once have been.

The session we have been discussing was Peetie's first in New York for more than two years. During it he also recorded his last "stomp," the one called *Shack Bully Stomp*. A shack bully was a job boss. As Danny Barker said of Ma Rainey, "'Ma,' that means the tops. That's the boss, the shack bully of the house. Not papa. Mama."[15]

> I used to play slow, but now I play it fast. (x2)
> Just to see the women shake their yas, yas, yas.
>
> Now I am a man that everybody knows. (x2)
> And you can see a crowd everywhere he goes.
>
> [spoken] Play it, boy.
>
> Rambled and I rambled till about the break of day. (x2)
> I think it's time, now, to stop my rambling ways.
>
> My name is Peetie, I'm on the line, you bet. (x2)
> I got something new that I ain't never told you yet.
>
> [spoken] Now, get down on it, boy. Beat it.

We are once again confronted with Peetie's arrogance and self-confidence, but it is important to look at those traits in terms not just of the kind of person Peetie was, but of the kind of person he wanted to be, and the kind of freedom and independence he wanted to have. Throughout this book I have tried to make it clear that in analyzing blues lyrics *desire* is a key word. Although many songs do not truly depict a singer's life in terms of concrete reality, they do often depict desire, frequently in open opposition to reality. Of course, some songs accurately reflected the circumstances of Peetie's life and the conditions under which he lived, but it is often the complexity of the woven strands themselves that constitute the marvelous in a blues, as we watch reality, desire, and fantasy construct a new pattern of imaginative fabric, one that sounds so familiar, yet we are sure we've never heard it before.

Thus, we can avoid a too-literal interpretation as well as an artificially metaphysical one, just as we must avoid the rigid formulas produced when blues and poetry are brought together in the light of dilettante academicism.

Another session with Lonnie and an unknown drummer took place on 18 October 1939, this time in Chicago. It was the last time Peetie played piano on his own records. The songs recorded included *Truckin' Thru Traffic*, *A Man Ain't Nothing But A Fool*, *Me No Lika You*, and the humorous *Hot Spring Blues*, sub-titled *Skin And Bones*. The nationally famous bathing spas at Hot Springs, Arkansas, often hird Blacks to wait upon and to serve healthful drinks to the rich whites who frequented such places, many of whom were victims of vague, indefinable illnesses. Peetie's song was quite comical:

> I got a little woman, she ain't nothing but skin and bones. (x2)
> But when I get my big money, oooh, well, well, right to Hot Springs she goes.
>
> Down in Hot Springs, she will get 200 baths a day. (x2)
> And when she come out, oooh, well, well, she won't be the same skinny way.
>
> Hot Springs is a place where all skinny people should be.
> Hot Springs is a place where all skinny people should go.
> And when they come out, oooh, well, well, they won't be skinny no more.
>
> Now take my advice, and don't treat your woman wrong. (x2)
> Because the woman that I got, oooh, well, well, she ain't nothing but skin and bones.
>
> Skin and bones, skin and bones, is your woman's fate. (x2)
> Well, now, you better take her to Hot Springs, oooh, well, well, now, before it is too late.

I have already mentioned that Peetie rarely relied on innuendo in his selection of material. The blues he recorded which were metaphorically sexual were, as *Black Horse Blues* indicates, more interesting than many songs of that genre.

> Woman, I got a black horse, and he rides just fine. (x2)
> I want you to come on over, oooh, well, well, and ride with me sometime.

He's a good riding horse, and he runs steady all the time. (x2)
Please come on over, oooh, well, well, now, and ride on this black horse of mine.

He's a good horse, and he trots so nice. (x2)
Now, if you ride him one time, oooh, well, well, you'll want to ride him all your life.

I know, once I lent my black horse to a lady friend. (x2)
And she said, "Please, mister, oooh, let me ride on that black horse again."

I'm gonna tell you women about that black horse of mine. (x2)
Please come up and see me, oooh, well, well, I'll let you ride that black horse some time.

The only other song recorded at that session was Sonny Boy Williamson's *Sugar Mama*—it was destined to become a blues standard.

Sugar mama, sugar mama, where did you get your sugar from? (x2)
You must have got that sweet sugar, oooh, well, well, from down on your man's sugar farm.

You got that fine sugar, sugar mama, and it's going right to my head. (x2)
And if you take it from me, sugar mama, oooh, well, well, I know I'll soon be dead.

Everybody's bragging 'bout your sugar, sugar mama, and I'm going bragging, too. (x2)
And if I can't get that sugar, mama, oooh, well, well, I don't know what I will do.

I can do without my coffee in the morning, but I must have my tea at night. (x2)
But when I want that sweet sugar, sugar mama, oooh, well, well, I don't feel just right.

That sugar you got, sugar mama, is going from town to town. (x2)
Everybody wants some of your sugar, mama, oooh, well, well, but please don't let them have more than four or five pounds.

DECCA RACE Records

PEETIE WHEATSTRAW
(BLUES SINGING)
7641 A Working Man's Blues / Easy Way Blues
7605 One To Twelve / Let's Talk Things Over
7589 Possum Den Blues / Road Tramp Blues
7578 Little Low Mellow Mama / Sinking Sun Blues

JOHNNIE TEMPLE
(BLUES SINGING WITH INST. ACC.)
7643 Good Suzie Down In Mississippi
7632 Up Today And Down Tomorrow / The Sun Goes Down In Blood
7599 If I Could Holler Getting Old Blues
7583 Better Not Let My Good Gal Catch You Here / Grinding Mill

THE HONEY DRIPPER
(ROOSEVELT SYKES, BLUES SINGING)
7655 New Mistake In Life / We Will Never Make The Grade
7642 Get Your Row Out / Under Eyed Woman
7612 Papa Low / Shoe Shiner's Moan
7597 Bitter Cup Blues / Love Will Wear You Down

GEORGIA WHITE
7652 How Do You Think I Feel / Do It Again
7596 Married Woman Blues / The Way I'm Feelin'
7562 The Blues Ain't Nothing But...? / My Worried Mind Blues
7608 Fire In The Mountain / When The Red Sun Turns To Gray

LOUIS JORDAN and his Tympany Five
7590 Flatfoot / Doug The Jitterbug
7609 Keep A Knockin' / At The Swing Cat's Ball
7623 Sam Jones Done Snagged His Britches / Swinging In The Cocoanut Trees

OLLIE SHEPARD and his Kentucky Boys
7651 Don't You Know / Li'l Liza Jane
7639 Blues 'Bout My Gal / Oh Maria
7629 Jelly Roll / Sweetest Thing Born

LEE BROWN
(BLUES SINGING)
7654 Lock And Key Blues / Treated Like A Dog
7626 I Can Lay It On Now / Decoration Day
7575 New Little Girl Little Girl / Moanin' Dove

A BROWN SKIN GAL IS THE BEST GAL AFTER ALL
Sung by **FAT HAYDEN** 7614

A Decca catalog supplement issued in 1939.

"Bring Me Flowers While I'm Living..."

From his recording session of 30 March 1939 onwards Peetie no longer accompanied himself. This has given rise to much speculation. He was frequently heard playing piano in the local clubs and bars until the end of his life, and his colleagues have asserted that he was in good health and certainly capable of playing on his own records. According to Harmon Ray, however, it was unpaid union dues that prevented Peetie playing on his own records, and this is indeed quite possible; a non-union musician could sing, but not play, in a union-controlled studio. However, if union problems were indeed the reason, Decca could easily have paid his union debt. Of course there may have been circumstances that prevented this, but if there were they are still obscure.

Some critics have suggested that Decca felt that Peetie's playing was becoming monotonous, and that a change of instrumentation might help boost sales, or at least maintain them. To be fair, one would have to concede that Peetie's playing could become tedious, especially in large doses. And his new accompanists gave the recordings a jazz flavor that earlier sessions lacked. On the other hand, the accompanists that replaced him and his usual crew managed to effect a musical monotony that was far duller than anything Peetie could ever have produced. Except when Lil Armstrong or Robert Lee McCoy contributed something imaginative, the rest of Peetie's records were musically uninspired. Burdened with accompanists whose cocktail sophistication bordered on the insipid, and depending on the rhythmic support of other musicians rather than his own, Peetie's voice sounded stiff. Regretfully, this trait was far from unnoticeable, and were it not for his remarkable flair for composition, Peetie's last recordings would hold no interest for us at all.

On the 30 March session Peetie was in New York. He was accompanied by Sam Price on piano, Teddy Bunn on guitar and O'Neil Spencer on drums. Each of these musicians was capable of producing imaginative music, and why they failed so completely on Peetie's records remains a mystery.

The first song of the session was *Possum Den Blues*.

It was early one morning when the possum left his den. (x2)

DECCA RACE RECORDS

NELSON, RED (Blues Singing)
7171 Crying Mother Blues
7154 Detroit Special
7185 Empty Bed Blues
7256 Gambling Man
7263 Girl I Left Behind
7136 Grand Trunk Blues
7263 Gravel In My Bed
7154 Long Ago Blues
7136 Slave Man Blues
7171 Streamline Train
7155 Sweetest Thing Born
7185 What A Time I'm Havin'
7155 When The Soldiers Get Their Bonus
7256 Who Put These Jinx On Me?

NORFOLK JAZZ QUARTET (Blues Singing)
7443 Beedle De Beedle De Bop Bop
7383 He Ha Shout
7349 Just Dream Of You
7349 Shim Sham Shimmie At The Crickets Ball
7333 Tell That Broad
7443 Suntan Baby Brown
7333 Swinging The Blues
7383 What's The Matter Now

NORFOLK JUBILEE QUARTET
7359 Didn't It Rain
7402 Free At Last
7421 My Feet Been Taken Out The Mirey Clay
7336 My Lord's Gonna Move This Wicked Race
7336 Pure Religion
7402 Sit Down, Sit Down, I Can't Sit Down
7421 'Way Down In Egypt Land
7359 You Got To Live So God Can Use You

ODOM, OLD CED & LIL "DIAMONDS" HARDAWAY
7247 Break 'Er Down—FT
7241 Derbytown—FT
7276 'Fore Day In The Morning—FT
7241 Hotter Than Fire—FT
7247 It's Your Yas Yas Yas—FT
7276 What You Gonna Do? FT

ORIGINAL ST. LOUIS CRACKERJACKS (Fox Trots)
7236 Blue Thinking of You
7265 Chasing The Blues Away
7236 Crackerjack Stomp
7248 Echo In The Dark
7248 Fussin'
7235 Good Old Bosom Bread
7265 Lonesome Moments
7235 Swing Jackson

OSCAR'S CHICAGO SWINGERS
7186 I Wonder Who's Boogiein' My Woogie Now
7201 My Gal's Been Foolin' Me FT
7186 New Rubbing On The Darned Old Thing
7201 Try Some Of That—FT

PAGE & HIS ORCHESTRA, HOT LIPS
7433 Down On The Levee—Blues Dance
7451 Good Old Bosom Bread—Blues
7451 He's Pulling His Whiskers—FT
7433 Old Man Ben—Blues Dance

PALMER, GLADYS (Singing and Pn)
7107 Get Behind Me Satan
7106 I'm Livin' In A Great Big Way
7106 In The Middle of A Kiss
7107 Trees

PALOOKA WASHBOARD BAND
7378 Back Door—Blues FT
7398 Save Me Some—Blues

7378 We Gonna Move—Blues FT
7398 You Done Tore Your Pants With Me

POWELL, TOMMY & HIS HI DE HO BOYS
7255 Got the Blues for Harlem—FT
7231 Hi De Ho Swing—FT
7255 Just About The Time—FT
7231 That Cat Is High—FT

PRINCE BUDDA & HIS BOYS (Prince Budda at the Vibraphone)
7363 In My Miz—FT
7363 When A Woman Gets The Blues—FT

ROBINSON, IKEY & HIS WINDY CITY FIVE
7430 Scrunch-Lo—FT
7430 Swing It—FT

SEGAR, CHARLIE (Keyboard Wizard Supreme)
7075 Boogie Woogie
7075 Cow Cow Blues
7027 Cuban Villa Blues
7027 Southern Hospitality

SHEPARD, OLLIE & HIS KENTUCKY BOYS (Blues Singing)
7448 Brown Skin Woman
7435 Drunk Again
7400 Honey Bee
7384 It It Ain't Love
7384 It's A Low Down Dirty Shame
7408 No One To Call You Dear
7435 One Woman Blues
7448 S-B-A- Blues
7408 She Walks Like A Kangaroo
7400 Sweetheart Land

SLEEPY JOHN ESTES (Blues Singing)
7354 Airplane Blues
7325 Down South Blues
7289 Drop Down Mama
7442 Floating Bridge
7414 Government Money
7354 Hobo Jungle Blues
7414 I Ain't Gonna Be Worried No More
7365 Jack and Jill Blues
7289 Married Woman Blues
7365 Need More Blues
7442 Poor Man's Friend (T Model)
7279 Someday Baby Blues
7325 Stop That Thing
7279 Who's Been Tellin' You Buddy Brown Blues

SMITH'S BURNING BUSH CONGREGATION, REV. NATHAN (Religious Services with Singing)
7148 Baptism At Burning Bush
7150 Collection Time
7150 Joining Church
7148 Lord's Supper

SMITH'S BURNING BUSH SUNDAY SCHOOL PUPILS, REV NATHAN (Preaching with Singing)
7112 Burning Bush Sunday School (2 Parts)

SMITH, WILLIE ("The Lion") & HIS CUBS
7086 Breeze—FT
7090 Echo of Spring—FT
7074 Harlem Joys—FT
7086 Sitting At The Table Opposite You—FT
7074 Streamline Gal—FT
7090 Swing, Brother, Swing—FT
7073 There's Gonna Be The Devil To Pay—FT
7073 What Can I Do With A Foolish Little Girl Like You—FT

TEMPLE, JOHNNIE and HARLEM HAMFATS
7456 County Jail Blues—Blues-FT
7444 Pimple Blues
7444 Mean Baby Blues-Blues-FT
7456 What Is That Smells Like Gravy—Blues-FT

THEARD, LOVIN' SAM (The Mad Comic) (Blues Singing)
7025 Rubbin' On The Darned Old Thing
7025 That Rhythm Gal
7146 Till I Die

TREMER, GEORGE H (Piano Novelty)
7120 Spirit of '49 Rag

UNCLE JOE DOBSON (Preaching with Singing)
7055 Kin You Take It
7124 My God Is A Rock In The Weary Land
7124 There Was A Man
7055 You Wooden Pistol You

UNCLE SKIPPER (Blues Singing)
7455 Look What a Shape I'm In (Bonus Blues)
7455 Twee Twee Twa

WHEATSTRAW, PEETIE (Blues Singing) (Th Devil's Son-In-Law)
7082 All Night Long Blues
7403 Baby Lou, Baby Lou
7272 Bengar Man Blues
7441 Ccke Alley
7123 C G A Train Blues
7144 Cocktail Man Blues
7159 Coun Can Shorty
7228 Country Fool Blues
7292 Crapshooter's Blues
7348 Crazy With The Blues
7167 Deep Sea Love
7472 Devilment Blues
7007 Doin' The Best I Can
7228 Drinking Man Blues
7272 Fairaxee Woman (Memphis Woman)
7243 False Hearted Woman
7167 First Shall Be Last and The Last Shall Be First
7391 Give Me Black or Brown
7061 Good Home Blues
7123 Good Hustler Blues
7453 Hard Headed Black Gal
7257 I Don't Want No Pretty Faced Woman
7422 I'm Gonna Cut Out Everything
7177 Kidnappers' Blues
7144 King Spider Blues
7257 Little House
7187 Meat Cutter Blues
7129 Lonesome Lonesome Blues
7200 Low Down Rascal
7187 Meat Cutter Blues
7379 New Working On The Project
7082 Number Blues
7187 Old Good Whiskey Blues
7292 Peetie Wheatstraw Stomp
7391 Peetie Wheatstraw Stomp No. 2
7177 Poor Millionaire Blues
7348 Ramblin' Man
7129 Santa Claus Blues
7403 Sick Bed Blues
7441 Slave Man Blues
7111 Sweet Lucille
7061 These Times
7379 Third Street's Going Down
7453 304 Blues (Lost My Job On the Project)
7018 Throw Me In The Alley
7243 When A Man Gets Down
7159 Ww I Get My Bonus
7111 Whiskey Head Blues
7200 Working Man
7311 Working On The Project
7311 Would You Would You Mama

WHISTLING BOB HOWE & FRANKIE GRIGGS (Blues Singing)
7085 Coldest Stuff In Town
7085 Hottest Stuff In Town

Alphabetical listing of Peetie's records, from the 1938 catalog (according to which every record Decca had ever issued in their "race" series was still available).

Decca catalog for 1938

About the same time, oooh, well, well, when my baby come
creeping in.

What makes you act like a possum when I ask you where
have you been? (x2)
You don't do nothing, oooh, well, well, but stand up there
and grin.

Peetie also recorded *Little Low Mellow Mama* and *A Working Man's Blues* (both average), and *Let's Talk Things Over* (dull). *One To Twelve* was a loosely-structured version of *The Dirty Dozens* that also seemed to draw on Kokomo Arnold's earlier hit, *Old Original Kokomo Blues*. The song contained the recurring phrase "just as sho," ("just as sure"), which was mistranscribed on the label as the subtitle *Just As Show*.

Just as sho' as one and one is two. (x2)
One time you drop a shuck on me, oooh, well, well, I'm
gonna drop one back on you.

Just as sho' as two and two is four. (x2)
If I leave you this time, oooh, well, well, I ain't coming
back to you no more.

Just as sho' as three and three is six. (x2)
I'm gonna learn you baby, oooh, well, well, how to get your
business fixed.

Just as sho' as four and four is eight. (x2)
When I get through with you, oooh, well, well, you will
keep your business straight.

Just as sho' as five and five is ten. (x2)
Baby I don't play no dozen, oooh, well, well, then please
don't ease me in.

Just as sho' as six and six is twelve. (x2)
If you ease me in the dozen, oooh, well, well, I'm bound to
ease you in hell.

One can easiley find oneself playing the Dozens almost against one's will, and what began as a simple joke can soon becomes a very unpleasant situation. The effortlessness of this transition is often alluded to in Dozens songs by the phrase "Don't ease me in." An extra shot of humor is added when the singer, who has been playing the Dozens throughout the song, insists "I don't play no Dozens."

Easy Way Blues dwelt on the hazards of a life of crime, while *Machine Gun Blues* was coupled with the later-recorded *Pocket Knife Blues* to provide a homogeneously violent record; unfortunately, neither song was very inspired. Probably the most engaging song of the session was *Sinking Sun Blues*:

> The evening sun is beginning to sink low. (x2)
> Just a few more hours, oooh, well, well, and I will have to go.
>
> Once I was going down the lonesome road. (x2)
> I met a man, oooh, well, well, and he was bound with a heavy load.
>
> By then the sun had turned the whole world red. (x2)
> Poor me didn't have no place, oooh, well, well, now, to lay my worried head.
>
> Darkness fell upon me, and I couldn't hear a sound. (x2)
> I let fate be my pillow, oooh, well, well, my bed be on the ground.
>
> When I think about all the bad deeds I have done. (x2)
> I say to myself, oooh, well, well, I'm no-good son-of-a-gun.

Some will think it grossly unfair of me to ascribe the authorship of this "poetic" song to someone other than Peetie, but I find it extremely unlikely that he wrote these stiff and traditionally pastoral verses, which lack any trace of emotion and spontaneity. They are devoid of all the inflected Wheatstrawisms that instantly branded a song as Peetie's own. It is also improbable that Charlie Jordan composed *Sinking Sun Blues*, and, although the composer credit is to "Bunch," a more likely nominee for the producer of this singular composition would be Sam Price or O'Neil Spencer.

On 14 September 1939 an unknown pianist and drummer replaced Price and Spencer; Bunn's replacement could hardly be heard; but he sounded a little like Lonnie Johnson. The harmonica player has long been thought to be Robert Lee McCoy, who definitely played on the 12 March 1941 date, but on this session the tone was much sweeter than McCoy's, and sounded more like that of Rhythm Willie [Hood], who recorded a few sides for OKeh in 1940. The session was uninspired, though *Beer Tavern* had moderately intriguing lyrics. *Rolling Chair* and *Love Bug Blues* could be ignored, as could *You Can't Stop Me From Drinking*. But *I Want Some Sea Food* was an inventive blues of the *double-entendre* type.

> I want some sea food, mama, and I don't mean no turnip greens. (x2)
> I want some fish, oooh, well, well, and you know just what I mean.
>
> I want fish, fish, mama, I wants it all the time. (x2)
> The peoples call it sea food, oooh, well, well, all up and down the line.
>
> If you love your sea food, you is a good friend of mine. (x2)
> If you don't love good fish, oooh, well, well, you better get on some kind of time.
>
> I want some sea food, mama, because I'm a sea food man. (x2)
> When I can't get my sea food, oooh, well, I goes to raising sand.
>
> So bye, bye, people, I hope this July will find you well. (x2)
> Because this sea food I'm talking about, oooh, well, well, now, I swear it is a burning hell.

Confidence Man was an extension of the theme so characteristic of the "stomps."

> You talk about confidence, I'm a confidence man from my birth. (x2)
> There's one thing sure, oooh, well, well, I can confidence every woman who lives on earth.

I got a woman take care of me, yes, she's just only sweet
sixteen. (x2)
I never done a day's work in my life, oooh, well, well, I
don't know even what work means.

Now work was made for two things, that was a fool and a
mule. (x2)
I wouldn't start to work, oooh, well, well, because I didn't
go to school.

Again we are confronted with the imaginatively extravagant constructions with which we are so familiar, yet one important implication of these themes remains undiscussed. What can be said about fantasy, historically and in general, can be said about fantasy in the blues. There is only space here for a short discussion, but the reader will find in the bibliography several works which provide a more thorough elucidation of the critical role of fantasy.

The imagination is one of the most powerful weapons that one can bring into action against the forces of repression. The joy and freedom created by imagination represent a demand for a future reality, and as such, a denial of the limitations imposed upon freedom by reality. The creation of a figure like the Devil's Son-in-Law was not only a protest against the drab role which the black man was expected to fill, but also a striking representation of what the future might hold. In the blues, as in life, it is the imagination that has the power to remind one insistently of what *can be*. The role of fantasy is a critical one, not a passively escapist one, and, since blues writers have been emphasizing only the latter role until now, it is time for a shift in perspective.

Confidence Man also provides us with one of those examples where fantasy and reality have merged one into the other. Unlikely though this statement is —"I never done a day's work in my life"—we cannot reason away Teddy Darby's testimony in support of it: "Peetie never did have a regular job 'cause he never needed one; he just always played around somewhere, just playing and singing, and I never known him to have a job."

When Peetie returned to the Decca studio in New York on 4 April 1940, he found himself in the company of drummer Sid Catlett, pianist Lil Armstrong, and trumpeter Jonah Jones. The same personnel was present for the next session on 28 August, and both sessions left everything to be desired. Even the lyrics were duller than usual; *Big Money Blues*, *Five Minutes Blues*, *Two Time Mama*, and *Pocket Knife Blues* were all unremarkable. *Big Apple Blues* did begin with a tantalizing image:

> Just look at that big apple rolling around in my bed.

Open Hearth Furnace at a Chicago Steel Mill.

Then there was *Chicago Mill Blues*:

> I used to have a woman that lived up on the hill. (x2)
> She was crazy about me, oooh, well, well, because I worked at the Chicago mill.

> You can hear the women hollering when the Chicago mill whistle blow. (x2)
> Cryin' "A-loose my man, oooh, well, well, please, and let him go."
>
> If you want a-plenty women, boys, work at the Chicago mill.(x2)
> You don't have to give them nothing, oooh, well, well, just tell them that you will.
>
> When I went to work, I worked at the Chicago mill. (x2)
> So I could get plenty women, oooh, well, well, at my free good will.
>
> So, bye, bye, boys, go on and have your thrill. (x2)
> You don't need no money, oooh, well, well, just say you work at the Chicago mill.

Peetie's attitude towards women hadn't changed—and, of course, he was taking advantage of the economic situation. The steel mills had always provided better than average pay, but one should not think that mill jobs for black workers were really plentiful in those days. It was possible for black people to get jobs at the mills, but mill executives have testified that their hiring practices of 1940 could hardly be described as non-discriminatory. (Indeed, until very recently, and possibly still, *women* were not allowed in the open-hearth areas of most mills.)

Peetie's recording of *Suicide Blues* was one of the few blues on that subject:

> My woman said she loved me, but she have packed her trunk and gone. (x2)
> I am going to commit suicide, oooh, well, well, if my baby don't come back home.
>
> We both made a vow that we never would part. (x2)
> But since she went away and left me, oooh, well, well, suicide is close to my heart.
>
> Now I love my baby, and I don't want her to stay away. (x2)

> I am bound to commit suicide, oooh, well, well, if she don't come back home to stay.
>
> When a man commits suicide, it is worry that's on his mind. (x2)
> Now when your good woman go and leave you, oooh, well, well, suicide is the best to find.

Peetie had alluded to suicide in *Long Lonesome Dive* and the ending of *Crazy With The Blues* contains a possible reference to suicide, also. Three such songs in a blues singer's arsenal of despair is unusual, but Peetie's work as a whole hardly hints at clinical depression, and everything we've heard about him suggests a more upbeat character.

Jaybird Blues is another composition whose authorship remains dubious. That apart, it is one of a type rarely recorded by any blues singer, and is certainly worth quoting.

> I waked up this morning, the sun was bright, you know. (x2)
> I said, "Come on, baby, oooh, well, well, you know it's time to go."
>
> The leaves is putting out and the birds begin to (build). (x2)
> I know that Spring is here, oooh, well, well, so I must be getting on up the hill.
>
> The bees is out in the forest, (sitting there) putting honey up in their comb. (x2)
> It is time to get my gal some money, oooh, well, well, so she will stay at home.
>
> You better get on some kind of time, because the pretty days will soon be gone. (x2)
> The winter will catch you, oooh, well, well, and you won't have a home.
>
> My clothes is all in pawn, and I haven't got a dime. (x2)
> It is my time to go, oooh, well, well, because I'm (reckless as a jaybird and wasting time).

The composer credit on this recording is to "Jordan," but a number of subtle factors suggest that Peetie could have been the author, and it is certainly more like his work than *Sinking Sun Blues*. All of Peetie's later material seems so unlike the earlier numbers that deciding which of the later songs were really Peetie's becomes an almost impossible task.

The next session was slightly better, although *Cuttin' 'Em Slow* and *Look Out For Yourself* were dull. In the latter song, Peetie made use of the *Sitting On Top Of The World* melody for at least the fourth time. *What's That?* was a version of the popular bawdy blues *What's That I Smell*, one version of which was recorded by Georgia Tom and Hannah May in 1930 (Perfect 170). *No 'Count Woman* was exceptional, at least in its initial verses :

> You fell for me, baby, but you only fell on my hands. (x2)
> And soon as you get tired of me, oooh, well, well, you will fall on some other man.
>
> When I picked you up, baby, you was beat just like a slave. (x2)
> You had one foot on a banana peeling, oooh, well, well, and the other foot in the grave.

But the most enticing song made that day was *Gangster's Blues*.

> Last night, buddy, I caught you kissing my wife.
> Don't you know I'm gonna take your life.
> I got the gangster blues. (x3)
> Boys, I am feeling mean.
>
> I'm going to take you for an easy ride.
> Drop you off on the river side.
> [refrain]
>
> I'm gonna bind your mouth so you can't talk.
> Tie your feet so you can't walk.
> [refrain]
>
> You can start your screaming, but must give in.

I'm gonna tear you to pieces, and put you back again.
[refrain]

Put up your hands and reach for the sky.
Gonna let you down before you bat an eye.
[refrain]

I'm gonna bury you out on the lone prairie.
Because I know you're (biting) on me.
[refrain]

One of the most attractive features of *Gangster's Blues* was that Peetie's knowledge of professional criminals seems to have come entirely from the mass media rather than first-hand experience. Thus "Put up your hands and reach for the sky," and "I'm gonna bury you out on the lone prairie!"

I Don't Feel Sleepy and *My Little Bit* were recorded at Peetie's next to last session, on 12 March 1941; with him were Robert Lee McCoy, harmonica, and possibly Lil Armstrong, piano. At this session he made his lyrically dullest coupling, *Love Me With Attention / You Got To Tell Me Something*, and although *I'm A Little Piece Of Leather* was not very good either, it was recorded eight years later by Herman "Peetie Wheatstraw" Ray. The two most interesting songs were *Seeing Is Believing* and *The Good Lawd's Children*. The former contained this somewhat philosophical verse :

This world is all right, it is the people that makes it bad. (x2)
You been believing everything you hear, oooh, well, well, it's no wonder you feel so sad.

There is no doubt that 1941 started out as a discouraging year for Peetie; more evidence of this can be found in the songs of his last session, but even this session contained the unusually pessimistic *The Good Lawd's Children*.

They say we are the lord's children, I don't say that ain't true. (x2)
But if we are the same like each other, oooh, well, well, why do they treat me like they do?

What's wrong with the lord's children, I don't understand. (x2)
Some men got no use for women, oooh, well, well, some women got no use for man.

I want to live on, children, soon I would just like to see. (x2)
What will become of us, oooh, well, well, by nineteen and fifty-three.

Some of the good lord's children, some of them ain't no good. (x2)
Some of them are the devil, oooh, well, well, and wouldn't help you if they could.

Some of the good lord's children (is about to) kneel and pray. (x2)
You serve the devil in the night, oooh, well, well, and serve the lord in the day.

The Good Lawd's Children was realistic as well as pessimistic, and, even if the second verse seems to refer to "women troubles," the note of social protest is inescapable. The reader will have to judge for himself whether the more direct protests, such as the above, have the same impact as the more poetic, and less direct, protests like the "stomps" or *Mister Livingood* (see below).

Peetie's last session was on 25 November 1941, less than a month before his death. He was accompanied by either Jack Dupree or Lil Armstrong on piano; Dupree himself has stated that he was present at that session, but the piano sounds nothing like him. Also a bass, and even a tenor saxophone accpompanied Peetie on three numbers. The session was quite remarkable, though a few mediocre tunes were recorded that day too. *Don't Put Yourself On The Spot* was not particularly noteworthy, while *Pawn Broker Blues* was the one remade years later by B. B. King.

I am a pawn broker, what do you want on your ring? (x2)
Every woman I loan, oooh, well, well, I'm loaning about the same old thing.

I'll have to use my tester see if it will stand the test. (x2)
I am a ring pawn broker, oooh, well, well, don't handle
    nothing but the best.

Eighteen carat is ok, fourteen carat won't make the grade.
    (x2)
I don't handle nothing oooh, well, well, but the best rings is
    made.

I'm a ring pawn broker, I pay the best price in town. (x2)
And if you don't believe me on my counting, oooh, well,
    well, now lay your ring down.

You may need money, lady, on your ring some day. (x2)
Can't ever tell, oooh, well, well, what bad luck may come
    your way.

The Good Lawd's Children was remade and left unissued. A fast-moving piano helped to make *Southern Girl Blues* wild and rollicking, and the lyrics remind one of the Peetie Wheatstraw of the mid-1930s.

I had a southern girl that used to please me so. (x2)
But she got to the place, oooh, well, well, I couldn't keep
    her in enough dough.

She made a great promise that she would treat me right.
    (x2)
But she went hog-wild, oooh, well, well, just in overnight.

She left the city, swelled her poor head. (x2)
I tried to get her to be good, but she got smart instead.

If you got a girl in the South, better go back where she's at.
    (x2)
Because these city slickers will get her wild as a bat.

Now this Chicago whiskey does them thataway.
Now this Chicago whiskey does something to their minds.
Women get jig-headed, oooh, well, well, they never drink
    moonshine.

> Now I know Chicago will get them that way. (x2)
> There's people coming to Chicago, oooh, well, well, going hog-wild every day.

Mister Livingood was one of Peetie's most fantastic creations:

> I am all snowed under and beat so bad. (x2)
> Not a dime, oooh, well, well, from the big wealth that I had.
>
> I could just 'phone anywhere in town. (x2)
> Mr Livingood wanted it, oooh, well, well, and they rush it down.
>
> I had a butler just to fetch me my gin. (x2)
> Living seven ways to the week, oooh, well, well, now, but I'm living ten.
>
> On big parties I drop money on the floor. (x2)
> And leave it for the sweeper, and walk on out the door.
>
> I buy my baby a silk dress everyday. (x2)
> She'd wear it one time, oooh, well, well, then she throw it away.
>
> I had money ( ), but I was too big a fool. (x2)
> I would throw it at the wind, oooh, well, because I was stubborn as a mule.

It was the same Peetie Wheatstraw, without a doubt. Although *Mister Livingood* didn't show it, an air of gloom pervaded the entire session. Peetie died accidentally twenty-six days later, yet, of the nine songs he recorded at his last session, four were about death. One was called *Separation Day Blues*:

> Ain't it hard to say goodbye on separation day. (x2)
> That's the last thing my baby said, oooh, well, well, when she walked away.
>
> I couldn't hardly take it, but I had the debt to pay. (x2)

Because my baby said goodbye, oooh, well, well, on separation day.

It was a hard pill to swallow, on that, going that way.
It is too late to holler, when your good girl is gone away.
It's a hard pill to swallow, oooh, well, well, when you think about separation day.

Wait here one hour while I go and pray. (x2)
I want to tell the people, oooh, well, well, I ain't seen (her?) myself today.

When you get up in the morning you don't have nothing to say. (x2)
Because your mind is resting, oooh, well, well, on separation day.

Another began "Old organ, you've played your last tune," and another was called *Hearse Man Blues*.

I wired my baby some flowers thinking I wouldn't get there in time. (x2)
The next telegram I received, oooh, well, well, that my baby was dying.

I walked around the casket and looked down in my baby's face. (x2)
Then I was soon on a wonder, oooh, well, well, what good woman would take her place.

The church bells began to tone, hearse wheels was rolling slow. (x2)
They are taking my baby to a place, oooh, well, well, where I won't see her no more.

Hearse driver, Mr Undertaker, Mr Hearseman please drive slow. (x2)
Well you are taking my baby, oooh, well, well, now, I swear we all is got to go.

Then I watched the undertaker slowly let her down. (x2)

If my baby don't go no further, oooh, well, well, I know
she's six feet in the ground.

Yet another was called *Bring Me Flowers While I'm Living.*

Bring me flowers whilst I'm living, please don't bring them
when I am dead. (x2)
And bring ice bags to my bedside, oooh, well, well, to cool
my aching head.

When a man is sick in bed, please come to my rescue. (x2)
When a man is dead and gone, oooh, well, well, how in the
world he know what you do.

Bring me water to my bed, a drink will keep me cool. (x2)
And just say after I have gone, oooh, well, well, "I sure
tried to help that fool."

I'll stay here as long as I can, leave when I can't help
myself. (x2)
We has all got to die, oooh, well, well, and I ain't no better
than no one else.

Don't bring me flowers after I'm dead, a dead man sure
can't smell. (x2)
And if I don't go to heaven, oooh, well, well, I don't sure
need no flowers in hell.

Less than a month later he was dead.

"They Came and Said Peetie Was Dead."

Peetie was killed in a car-train collision at 11.30 a.m. on his birthday on Sunday, 21 December 1941. The car in which he was riding was being driven south on Third Street when it failed to make a curve, left the road, and struck a standing freight car. The accident occurred just south of Illinois Avenue, less than a block from Peetie's home. He died in hospital four hours later.

The local blues community was stunned. "It was a big thing when Peetie Wheatstraw died," said Henry Townsend. "A lot of people took that pretty hard. At the time of [his] death, he and Walter Davis were about the most popular people. They were the two most popular people in the city of St Louis....Peetie was in his bloom."[16]

Among the newspapers reporting the event the next day were the *St Louis Globe-Democrat*, which identified Peetie only as "William Bunch," an "East St Louis negro," and the *East St Louis Metro-Journal*, which reported the accident in full and even supplied an account of Peetie's musical career. Of the music trade publications, both *Variety* (on 31 December) and *Billboard* (on 10 January) published short death notices in their obituary columns. On 15 January *Down Beat* gave Peetie the recognition he deserved; the notice of his death was run at at the top of the front page. Above the story was the headline, "Blues Shouter Killed After Waxing *Hearseman Blues*."

Teddy Darby and Big Joe Williams were Peetie's close friends, and both of them were affected quite strongly by his death. Their recollections of the accident conflict with each other as well as with the newspapers' version, but, since each of their accounts is probably more true than false, they are definitely worth repeating. Here is how Teddy Darby remembered the morning of 21 December:

We'd been sitting here awhile. That wasn't here, of course. Then, in those day, I was living at 2135 Kansas Avenue [in East St Louis]. And we were drinking, you know. And they had this Buick; Peetie and this other guy. I don't remember his name. It was the other guy's car, though. But they had this Buick, and Peetie says, "Let's go." He says to me, "C'mon, let's go blow

Monday, December 22, 1941

Three Negroes Die in Auto, Train Crash

Musician, Two Companions Killed; City Fatalities Now 22

William Bunch, 39, a Negro, known to "jive" fans as "Peetie Wheatstraw," and two companions were killed at 11:30 a.m. Sunday when an automobile traveling at a high speed crashed into the rear end of Louisville & Nashville Railroad Co. freight train standing on a siding at Third street and Illinois avenue. Bunch lived at 468A North Third street.

One other person was killed in an accident near Columbia, making the traffic toll in this area four for the week-end. The deaths of the three Negroes in Third street raised the East St. Louis traffic toll to 22 for the year in comparison with 19 at this time last year. The county total now is 84. At the same time last year it was 79.

Two Die Instantly

Killed with Bunch were Romie Self, 41, a Negro, 320 Winstanley avenue, a packing house worker, driver of the car, and Will Rainey, 42, of 222 North Third street, a chipper in the Commonwealth Steel Co. plant at Granite City. Self and Rainey were killed instantly and Bunch died at 4:20 p.m.

All three men were thrown from the car by the impact that moved 16 freight cars on the siding.

Wife Sees Crash

Bunch's widow was a witness to the accident. She said she was seated in the window of her home less than a block away from the scene of the crash. She said she saw the speeding car hit the box cars but was unaware her husband was involved until she ran to the scene.

Bunch, under the name of Peetie Wheatstraw, wrote and played music that was recorded. Included in the music he has written and played is "Suicide Blues," "Cuttin 'Em Slow," "Gangster Blues," and the "Devil's Son-in-Law." His picture appears on advertisements of a record company as a guitar and piano player.

Police obtained an account of the accident from Leo Mullins, 38, of 445 North Fourteenth street, an employe of the L. & N. He said he saw the car traveling south in Third street "60 or 65 miles an hour."

The car went up an embankment at a curve in Third street and hit the end of the box cars. Mullins said the boxcars moved 25 feet when the automobile hit them.

From The East St Louis Metro-Journal.

Big Joe Williams knew Peetie well.

this Buick out." I remember that. I don't know—I didn't know whether I should go, but I asked my wife if I could go and she said, "No." She wanted me to stay home with her, so I stayed home and they left. No, there wasn't nobody but Peetie and the guy that owned the car—that was all, just them two. And then, just half an hour later, they came and said Peetie was dead. And he was just here.

It was in 1964 when I first asked Big Joe about Peetie's death; in 1969, his story was the same:

Me and Peetie were in this big car—him and me were in the back and he had a guitar; he was playing *61 Highway*, I never will forget that. It was just before Christmas. And there were two guys in front, one of them owned the car. Rainey and Romie, big-time gamblers, Rainey and Romie. And I was drunk and I got evil, just evil, you know. And I got out to go home. See, we was in East St Louis at the time, but I lived in St Louis, across the river. So I got out to catch a streetcar back to St Louis. I was home in bed and Walter Davis came over. See, he'd seen us earlier so he thought I was in the wreck. So he told Mary, "Joe's dead," and I was right there. Mary said, "He ain't dead, 'cause he's right here, drunk." I got up and came out and Walter said, "Well, Peetie's dead." And I said, "No, he ain't, 'cause I was just with him." and Walter said, "Hell, he ain't. He's dead. I've just come from there. They had a wreck." He was right, too, they were all dead, except Peetie lived a few hours, but he died, too.

Peetie's body was shipped to Cotton Plant, Arkansas, where he was buried. For a while it looked as though he was going to be more dead than most. The blues revival, when it began, can hardly be said to have concentrated on '30s St Louis piano players. From Gus Cannon and Blind Lemon Jefferson to Willie McTell and Elmore James, or from Charley Patton and Robert Johnson to Howlin' Wolf and Muddy Waters, there wasn't much room for Peetie Wheatstraw. Paul Oliver wrote an article on Peetie as early as 1956, and he quoted him widely in his other works, but other writers virtually ignored him He was also ignored by the collecting establishment, which preferred guitars to pianos and Gennetts to Deccas.

Blues Shouter Killed After Waxing 'Hearseman Blues'

by ONAH SPENCER

Chicago—Less than one month after he recorded *Give Me Flowers While I'm Livin'* and *Hearseman Blues*, Peetie Wheatstraw, famous blues singer, was killed when the car in which he and two others were riding was struck by a passenger train. The accident occurred in St. Louis, Dec. 21.

Wheatstraw, whose real name was William Bunch, was known by his own descriptive titles as The Devil's Son-in-law and the High Sheriff of Hell. Born thirty-six years ago in Little Rock, Ark., Wheatstraw started recording blues for Decca as early as 1926 and it was estimated that Peetie had cut some 400 sides to date. He originated the long shout "whooee" used by so many blues singers today and with his singing played either guitar or piano.

Wheatstraw was one of the few blues chanters to stay on wax throughout the depression along with such stars as Bessie Smith and LeRoy *How Long, How Long Carr*. A few of his better known sides are, *Workin' on the Project, Doin' the Best I Can* and *304 Blues*. Peetie is survived by his wife, Lizzie Bunch.

Comes Through With a Baby Boy

On the Cover

The Bobby Byrne Little Theater and Music for Special Occasions group posed for the tableau on *Down Beat's* cover. The Byrne ork is currently at Chicago's Hotel Sherman. The actors from left to right are Don Byrne, Bobby's brother and saxophonist; Walt McGuffin, trombone player; Dick Farrel, drums; vocalist Dorothy Claire and boss Bobby. Pic by *Rudy Weis*; idea by *Eddie Beaumonte*.

Then Chris Strachwitz of Arhoolie Records issued an LP on his Blues Classics label with eight tracks by Peetie and eight by Kokomo Arnold. The picture on the cover was the one that seems to be Harmon Ray, but in those days no one knew it wasn't Peetie. German Brunswick issued a Peetie EP, but three of the four tracks were from later Decca sessions. A white-label LP with seventeen tracks by Peetie was issued only in Europe as a limited edition, and there were six sides reissued on the Sunflower label. Besides the above, the Down With The Game label issued an LP with a number of Peetie's songs on it, and there were a few scattered anthology appearances.

Since then, things have improved steadily. Although the United States still had not produced an LP of Peetie's work [by 1970], Saydisc, in Great Britain, issued a two-volume set of thirty-two of Peetie's recordings. On the cover of one LP is the standard photograph of Peetie from the Decca catalogue; on the other is the photograph of Harmon Ray. He has fared better in the CD era, largely due to Document which has reissued all of his songs, but Catfish and Fremeaux and have also issued worthwhile CDs..

Perhaps Peetie was destined to be surrounded with confusion. Although a number of articles about him exist, they have revealed only tiny fragments of his story. To remedy that lack of concrete facts was one of my motives for writing this book; I had others, as well. To unravel part of the mystery that cloaked the figure known as the Devil's Son-in-Law; to reveal, in all his grandeur and passion, Peetie Wheatstraw as a person as well as a maker of songs; to uncover those powers that are inherent in the blues, but are so rarely recognized or discussed; all these were my intentions. Yet I am inclined to think that, as facts emerge and as the picture draws closer to completion, the romance, mystery, and power that have always surrounded Peetie, his songs, and indeed the blues as a whole, tend only to increase, while the subjects with which we deal are stripped of their vagaries and revealed in their true light. For what stands then is often what one could only have dreamed, and dreaming has always been our only hope.

Beth & Paul Garon: *The Death of Peetie Wheatstraw: What Really Happened.*

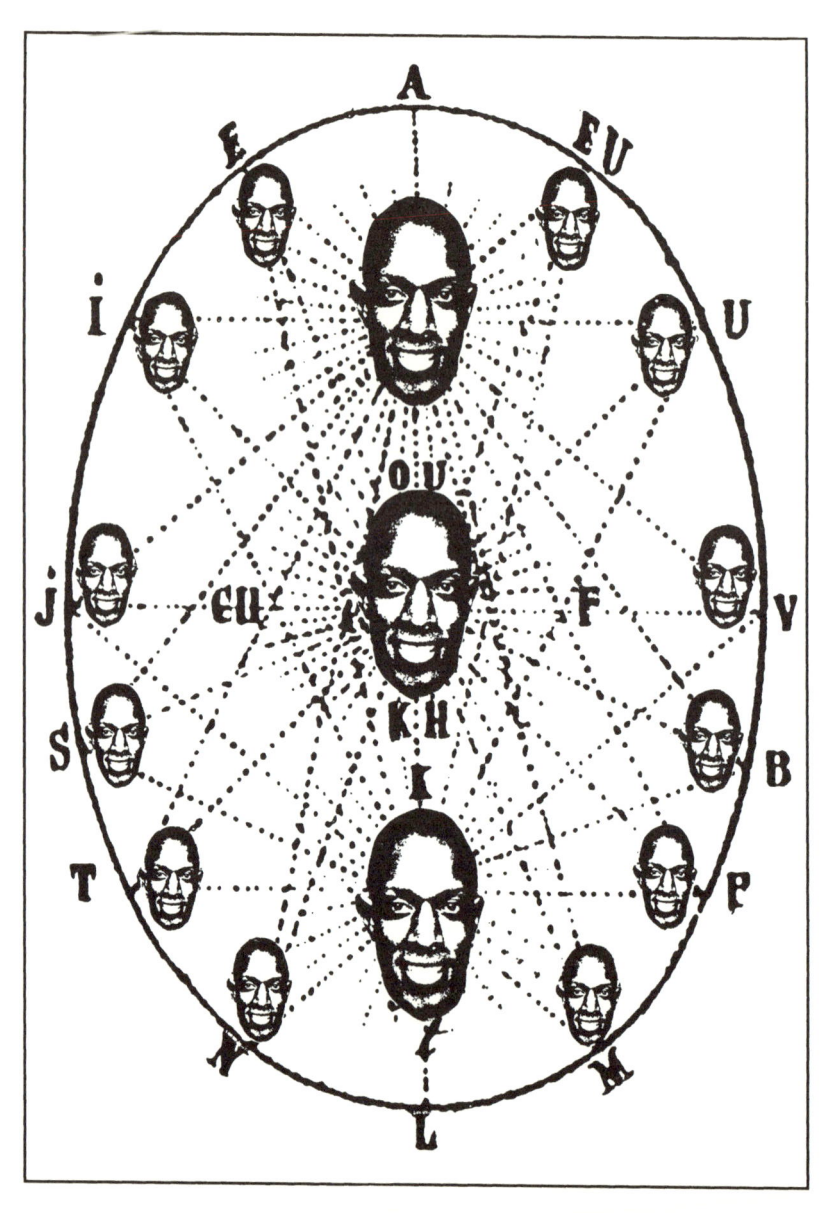

Franklin Rosemont: *The Luciferian Gesture, or The Origin of Song*

"So My Evil Spirit Won't Hang Around Your Door"

(*Afterword: 2002, 100th anniversary of Peetie's birth*)

While the manuscript for *The Devil's Son-in-Law* was at the publisher's, but before the book came out—around 1970—I had received a dust jacket proof from the publisher. I carried it around with me as a research tool. On a southern record-hunting trip, I made a detour to Cotton Plant, Arkansas, where Peetie is buried, to see what information I could find on Peetie Wheatstraw. I stopped at the first funeral home I saw, but the staff told me they wouldn't know anything about the burial of a dead "colored man." They sent me to a corner garage to "ask around."

Several African American men fielded my query and then disappeared into the garage itself. When they didn't come out, I went in myself. A group of seven men were talking about Peetie Wheatstraw. They didn't know much, but they all remembered him. He had died 30 years earlier so this wasn't unusual. "You might go over to that house," said one pointing to another street. "His brother Sam lives there." That was the first I'd heard of a brother so I dashed over there immediately.

A middle-aged woman sat on the porch, separated from me by about 20 feet of yard and a fence.

From the other side of the fence, I said that I was looking for relatives of William Bunch. Not a word in reply, so I repeated my question. I was still met with silence. Finally I said, "I'm looking for anyone who knew Peetie Wheatstraw." The woman's head whipped up in my direction, and she turned to the house, shouting, "Sam, Sam, there's a man out here wants to talk about Peetie Wheatstraw."

A very elderly Sam Bunch, brother of William, descended the steps and came to the gate. I showed him the cover of the book, but he wasn't deeply impressed. He may even have been angered that the sinning brother would get so much more attention than the righteous one. Had I broken Christianity's promise of a reward? Sam had told Peetie many times to quit playing the blues and return to Cotton Plant and the church, but Peetie paid him no mind. Other than that, Sam had little to say about Peetie.

Thirty-one years later, a St Louis disk-jockey named Robert Stolle made the same journey. He started at a cafe instead of a funeral home, and was directed to a white man named Buck who was in his eighties and remembered everyone. Buck led them around the corner to a garage (!), where a bunch of elderly African American men were sitting. When he told the men that Stolle was looking for information about Peetie Wheatstraw, one man yelled, "The Devil's Son-in-Law" and another laughed and said, "Yeah, the High Sheriff of Hell." The garage gang didn't have a lot of specific information to pass on, but one can't help thinking, were these the same guys I saw in 1970?

Stolle was directed to the house of a fellow whose father was a guitar player and friend of Peetie's. Indeed, he had occasionally played with Peetie and even had a major marital spat over spending too much time in Wheatstraw's company. Interestingly, this man, as well as the garage group, only remember Peetie as a guitar player.

When Peetie died and his body was sent to Cotton Plant, his father, a deacon in the local church, made it very clear that he did not approve of Peetie's life. Nonetheless, he would allow him to be buried in the church cemetery since he *was* indeed his son. In spite of the fact that a number of Bunch family graves had tombstones, Peetie's does not. Nor is he in the main (back) part of the cemetery with the rest of the family, but rather out front, near the road.

* * *

These days, when you hear about the Devil and the blues, you usually hear about Robert Johnson. Indeed, the Royal Robert has captured the public's imagination to such an extent that you would think he owned the Devil himself, if not vice-versa. Yet we know the "blues singer at the crossroads" legend was also personally seized upon by Tommy Johnson, another legendary bluesman from an earlier generation. Robert Johnson was at least a second generation country blues artist, having learned from Son House and Charlie Patton, and even Peetie Wheatstraw.

Indeed, Peetie may have been the main factor in popularizing the connection between blues singers and the Devil, a connection that needed no emphasis in parts of the African American community for which blues singers were the designated spokespersons. Peetie's records were labeled "Peetie Wheatstraw (The Devil's Son-in-Law)" beginning in September 1930, right after his Summer 1930 career start in a duet with "Neckbones."

We don't even know that Robert Johnson's alleged association with the Devil was very well known beyond the circle of his immediate colleagues. It may have been; we don't know. But we do know that Peetie Wheatstraw was so well known as The Devil's Son-in-Law that decades after his death, members of the original listening community responded with "Yeah, the Devil's Son-in-Law" when Peetie's name was mentioned. As we mentioned earlier, Peetie's Bluebird session even resulted in the issuing of one record titled *Devil's Son-in-Law*. Over and over again, the association of Peetie with the Devil was hammered into his public's consciousness.

Only once did the appellation "The High Sheriff from Hell" appear on a record, but Peetie was known by that name as well, and he refers to himself as "The High Sheriff from Hell" on *Peetie Wheatstraw Stomp*. These designations gave Peetie a sense of power, opposition, and resistance and it gave his listener's a figure of great majesty with whom they could identify.

Peetie's alliance with the Devil is in keeping with what we know of blues as the Devil's music. Peetie performed no gospel songs and stayed out of church. If he had religion at all, it may have been as Iva Smith sang in 1927—"I rubbed my palm, prayed to the jack of spades " (*Barrel House Mojo*, Paramount 12472). He never announced his intention to become a minister in his declining years, although admittedly, his years declined rather suddenly at the end.

The Devil, as a sign of Evil, couldn't help but conjure up a sympathetic feeling among those listeners who felt that as African Americans in a white world, they needed an *agent of opposition* to carry on through their lives. For so many, God was an agent of accomodation, and if the Black church began to play a greater leadership role in the civil rights era, it is no accident that African American music turned away from the Devil at precisely this point, insisting on a more organized opposition than was the Devil's habit. Progress often first appears as Evil, wrote Hegel, and I like to think that the oppositional consciousness that inspired so many during the 1960s saw its first bloom in the words of the blues singers.

* * *

No assessment of Peetie could be complete without acknowledging some of the negative aspects of his recorded legacy. In spite of my love for Peetie, I know there are others who don't share my fondness for his style, and believe me, I do understand. By 1938, when he wasn't accompanied by Kokomo Arnold, and when he wasn't playing an unusual piece like *Shack Bully Stomp,* Peetie's piano accompaniment could get boring.

The chief Peetie Wheatstraw hater might be the late Nick Perls, founder of Yazoo records, who is credited with saying, only half-jokingly, that Peetie Wheatstraw "single-handedly ruined blues singing." What did Perls mean by this sweeping denunciation? That the advent of Peetie heralded the demise of all the great rough-voiced country blues guitarists of the 1920s and their style of playing? No more Charlie Patton, Son House, Tommy Johnson, or Ishman Bracey. Memphis Minnie lived on, but she did so with pianos, drums, and horns, not with solo acoustic guitars. So Robert Johnson and Bukka White notwithstanding, Peetie ruined everything!

This notion is an interesting one, beyond its enshrinement as the ultimate rural acoustic guitar elitism. The Wheatstraw style was a smooth, citified style that did seem to dominate the blues in the 1930s, and Wheatstraw was very influential, as we have seen. On the other hand, Peetie was one of many popularizers of a style of singing that was made fashionable by Leroy Carr in 1928. Carr's *How Long, How Long, Blues* probably sold more copies than any record ever made by Peetie, and he introduced his style several years before Peetie every made a record. Indeed, Carr and Blackwell had recorded dozens of songs for Vocalion before Peetie made his debut on that label in 1930.

The style Perls identified so closely with Peetie was shared, throughout the thirties, with considerably less excitement, by Bumble Bee Slim and Little Bill Gaither and they had lengthy careers, especially the former who recorded in the LP era. Walter Davis, a fairly urbanized piano player and somewhat bland singer and a friend of Wheatstraw's, began recording before Peetie and continued to record well after Peetie's death.

This was the style of the era, and Peetie could well have been it's most popular exponent, but if this is the case, he should be judged by the majesty of his own performances, not the intentsity of one's mourning for an age gone by.

Decca catalog for 1940

NOTES

[1] Thanks to the indefatigable Bob Engle for locating the Bunch family data in the 1920 census.

[2] Jim O'Neal, Amy Van Singel, eds, *Voice of the Blues. Classic Interviews from Living Blues Magazine* (New York: Routledge, 2002), 87.

[3] Ibid., 53-54.

[4] Henry Townsend and Bill Greensmith, *A Blues Life* (Urbana: University of Illinois Press, 1999), 62.

[5] Ibid., 60, 61.

[6] F. Jack Hurley and David Evans, "Bukka White," in *Tom Ashley, Sam McGee, Bukka White. Tennessee Traditional Singers* (Knoxville: University of Tennessee Press, 1981), 170.

[7] Townsend and Greensmith, *A Blues Life*, 56.

[8] Tony Russell, "The Deputy High Sheriff from Hell, Harmon Ray," *Living Blues*, no. 26 (March-April 1976): 14-15.

[9] Robert G. O'Meally, "How Can the Light Deny the Dark," *Atlantic Monthly* 244, no. 1 (July 1999): 89-94, Http://www.theatlantic.com/issues/99jul/9907ellison.htm.

[10] Barbara Foley, "Ralph Ellison as Proletarian Journalist" (1999), Http://newark.rutgers.edu~bfoley/foleyreleft2.html.

[11] Foley, "Ralph Ellison as Proletarian Journalist"

[12] Houston Baker, "Failed Prophet and Falling Stock: Why Ralph Ellison Was Never Avant-Garde," *Stanford Humanities Review* 7, no. 1 (1999), Http://www.stanford.edu/group/SHR/7-1/html/body_baker.html.

[13] David Honeyboy Edwards, *The World Don't Owe Me Nothing* (Chicago: Chicago Review Press, 1997), 116.

[14] Angela Davis, *Blues Legacies and Black Feminism: Ma Rainey, Bessie Smith and Billie Holiday* (New York: Pantheon, 1998).

[15] Quoted in the film "Wild Women Don't Have the Blues." Produced by Carole van Falkenburg and Christine Dall, 1969. Calliope Productions.

[16] Henry Townsend and Bill Greensmith, *A Blues Life* (Urbana: University of Illinois Press, 1999), 61-62.

BIBLIOGRAPHY

Baker, Houston. "Failed Prophet and Falling Stock: Why Ralph Ellison Was Never Avant-Garde." *Stanford Humanities Review* 7, no. 1 (1999). Http://www.stanford.edu/group/SHR/7-1/html/body_baker.html.

Broonzy, Big Bill, as told to Yannick Bruynoghe. "Who Got the Money?" *Living Blues*, no. 55 (Winter 1982–83): 21.

Dixon, Robert, and John Godrich. *Recording the Blues.* New York: Stein and Day, 1970.

Ellison, Ralph. *Invisible Man.* New York: Random House, 1952.

Foley, Barbara. "Ralph Ellison as Proletarian Journalist," 1999. *Http://newark.rutgers.edubfoley/foleyreleft2.html.*

Garon, Paul. "Peetie Wheatstraw." *Blues Unlimited*, no. 20 (March 1965).

———. "The Streets of Louisville and Peetie Wheatstraw." *Blues Unlimited*, no. 29 (January 1966).

———. "Blues and the Poetry of Revolt." *Arsenal: Surrealist Subversion*, no. 1 (1970).

———. "The Devil's Son-in-Law." *Radical America*, January 1970.

———. "Blues and the Church: Revolt and Resignation." *Living Blues*, no. 1 (Spring 1970).

———. "Lucifer's Laughter: The Domain of Peetie Wheatstraw." *Marvelous Freedom/Vigilance of Desire,* Catalog of the World Surrealist Exhibition. Chicago. Gallery Black Swan, 1976, 20.

O'Meally, Robert G. "How Can the Light Deny the Dark." *Atlantic Monthly* 244, no. 1 (July 1999): 89-94. *Http://www.theatlantic.com/issues/99jul/9907ellison.htm.*

O'Neal, Jim, and Amy Van Singel, eds. *Voice of the Blues.; Classic Interviews from Living Blues Magazine.* New York: Routledge, 2002.

Odum, Howard W., and Guy B. Johnson. *The Negro and His Songs.* Chapel Hill: University of North Carolina Press, 1925.

Oliver, Paul. "Devil's Son-in-Law." *Music Mirror,* March 1956.

———. "Peetie Wheastraw." *Jazz Monthly* 5, no. 3 (May 1959).

Peetie's Application for Social Security Account Number.

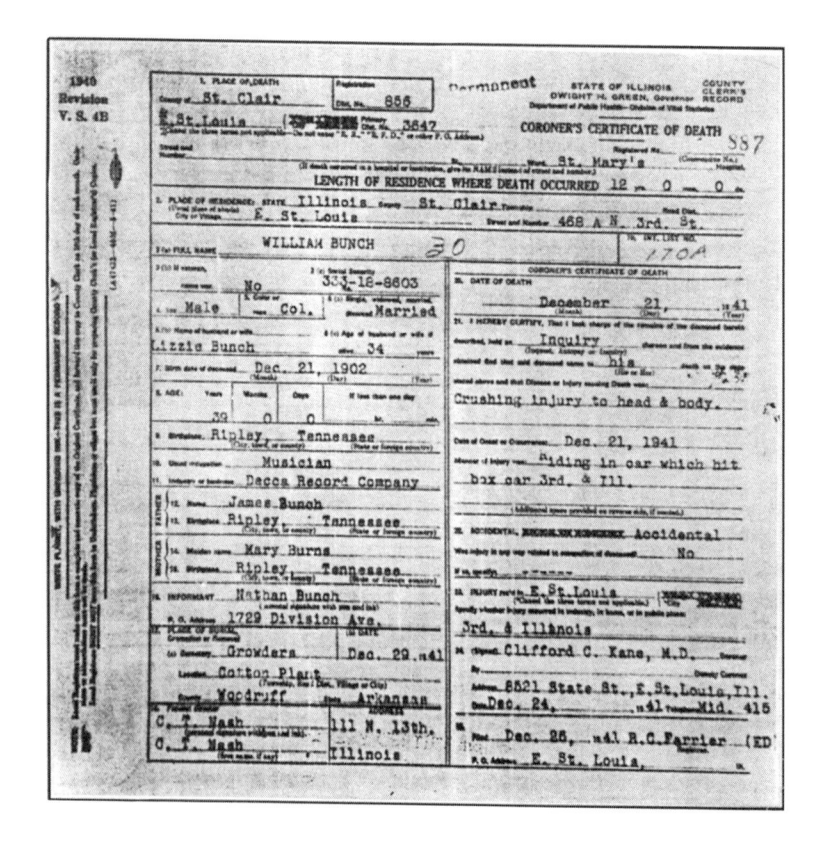

———. "Kokomo Arnold." *Jazz Monthly* 8, no. 3 (May 1962).

———. *Conversation with the Blues*. London: Cassell, 1965.

———. *Screening the Blues* [US Title: *Aspects of the Blues Tradition*.] London: Cassell, 1968.

———. *The Story of the Blues*. Philadelphia: Chilton Book Company, 1969.

Pierson, Leroy. "St Louis Blues." *Living Blues,* no. 3 (Fall 1970).

Rosemont, Franklin. "Preliminary Reconnaissance of Surrealist Cultural Revolution." *Surrealist Insurrection,* no. 3 (August 1968).

Rudwick, Elliott M. *Race Riot in East St Louis, July 2, 1917.* Cleveland: World, 1969.

Russell, Tony. "The Deputy High Sheriff from Hell, Harmon Ray." *Living Blues,* no. 26 (March–April 1976): 14–15.

Beth Garon: *The Devil's Son-in-Law*
(drawn in Lipstick, Blusher and Foundation).

DISCOGRAPHY

This discography is based on that in *Blues and Gospel Records 1890-1943*, and is reproduced by courtesy of the authors, John Godrich, R. M. W. Dixon, and Howard Rye.

The following label abbreviations are used: M ARC (American Record Company, including the Banner, Melotone, Oriole, Perfect, and Romeo labels), BB (Bluebird), Cq (Conqueror), De (Decca), and Vo (Vocalion). Original 78rpm issues are in **bold**. A key to the LP and CD reissues appears at the end of this discography.

Other abbreivations include: acc. (accompanied); dms (drums); gtr (guitar); hc (harmonica); pno (piano); sbs (string bass); stl gtr (steel guitar); ten (tenor sax); tpt (trumpet); and vcl (vocal).

While every attempt has been made to make this discography comprehensive, I have not tried to list every issue in every country. The 1969 LP *The Story of the Blues*, for example, was issued in the US, Australia, Czechoslovakia, Germany, etc., all with different issue numbers. I have recorded here only the original UK issue. Many issues are also reissued —often more than once–on budget labels, and I have made no attempt to list these multiple appearances.

Vcl duets with "Neckbones" acc by own piano; prob "Neckbones," gtr; unknown sbs.

Chicago, 13 August 1930

C-6098-A ***Tennessee Peaches Blues*** (Fields-Bunch)**Vo 1552, 04443**; Wolf WSE 115, Wolf WSE 118, Down With The Game D 204, Document DOCD-5241

C-6099-A ***Four O'Clock In The Morning***, (Fields-Bunch) **Vo 1552**; Wolf WSE 115, Wolf WSE 118, Document DOCD-5241

Acc by own pno; prob Charlie Jordan, gtr-1.

Chicago, 19 September 1930

C-6161-A ***School Days***-1 (Bunch) **Vo 1569**; Old Tramp OT 1216, Document DOCD-5241

C-6162-A ***So Soon***-1 (Bunch) **Vo 1569**; Old Tramp OT 1216, Document DOCD-5241

C-6402-A ***Don't Feel Welcome Blues*** (Bunch) **Vo 1597, 04443**; RST BD-2011, Down With The Game D 204, Document DOCD-5241

C-6403-A ***Strange Man Blues*** (Bunch) **Vo 1597**; Old Tramp OT 1216, Document DOCD-5241

Acc by own pno; Charlie Jordan, gtr; unknown sbs-1.

Chicago, 4 November 1930

C-6486-A ***So Long Blues*** (Bunch) **Vo 1620**; Down With The Game D 204, Document DOCD-5241

C-6487-A ***Mama's Advice***-1 (Bunch) **Vo 1620, 04487, Cq 9201**; Blues Classics BC4, Document DOCD-5241

C-6488-A ***Ain't It A Pity And A Shame*** (Bunch) **Vo 1649, 04733, Cq 9277**; Saydisc SDR191, CBS 52797, Document DOCD-5241, Blues Collection EPM 15839-2

C-6489-A ***Don't Hang My Clothes On No Barb Wire Line*** (Bunch) **Vo 1649, 04733, Cq 9277**; Saydisc SDR191, Mamlish S-3805, Pigmeat PM 002, Document DOCD-5241

Acc by own pno; Charlie Jordan, gtr.

Chicago, 6 January 1931

C-6891-A *C And A Blues* (Bunch) **Vo 1672, 04592;** Saydisc SDR191, Origin OJL20, Document DOCD-5241
C-6892- *Six Weeks Old Blues* Vo unissued

Chicago, 17 March 1931

VO-146-A *Six Weeks Old Blues* (Bunch) **Vo 1672;** Old Tramp OT 1216, Document DOCD-5241, Catfish 107

Acc by own pno; poss Charlie McCoy, gtr.

Chicago, 28 September 1931

67560-1 *Devil's Son-In-Law* (Wheatstraw) **Bluebird B5451**; Old Tramp OT 1216, RCA (J) RA-5433/5, RCA (F) PM 42039, Blues Collection BLU NC 082, Document DOCD-5241, Fremeaux FA-255
67561-1 *Pete Wheatstraw* (Wheatstraw) **Bluebird B5451**; Old Tramp OT 1200, RCA (J) RA-5433/5, Blues Collection BLU NC 082, Document DOCD-5241, Fremeaux FA-255, Bluebird 09026-63988-2 (as *Peetie Wheatstraw*)
67566-1 *Creeping Blues* (Wheatstraw) **Bluebird B5626**; Old Tramp OT 1216, Document DOCD-5241
67567-1 *Ice And Snow Blues* (Wheatstraw) **Bluebird B5626**; Blues Classics BC 4, Document DOCD-5241, Yazoo 2061, Indigo 2076
NOTE: Above Bluebird issues as by "Pete Wheatstraw"

Acc by own gtr.

New York, 15 March 1932

11492-A *Police Station Blues* (Wheatstraw) **Vo 1722, 04487, Cq 9201,** Old Tramp OT 1216, Columbia C4K 47911, Charly CD DIG 18, Blues Collection BLU NC 082, Document DOCD-5241
11493-A *All Alone Blues* (Wheatstraw) **Vo 1722, 04912, Cq 9767,** Old Tramp OT 1216, Document DOCD-5241

New York, 17 March 1932

11518-A *Can't See Blues* (Wheatstraw) **Vo 1727, 04912,** Old Tramp OT 1216, Document DOCD-5241
11519-A *Sleepless Nights Blues* (Wheatstraw) **Vo 1727, 04592;** Saydisc SDR191, Origin OJL20, Yazoo L-1030, Document DOCD-5241

Acc by own pno; prob Charlie Jordan, gtr.

Chicago, 25 March 1934

CP-1061-3 *Back Door Blues* (-) **Vo 02783;** Document DOCD-5242
CP-1062- *My Baby Blues* Vo unissued
CP-1063-2 *Packin' Up Blues* (-) **Vo 02783;** Document DOCD-5242
CP-1064-1 *Long Lonesome Dive (Long Lonesome Drive.)* (-)**Vo 02712, Cq 8850, ARC 7-04-79;** Old Tramp OT 1200, Down With The Game D 204, Document DOCD-5242
CP-1065-3 *Midnight Blues* (-) **Vo 03155;** Old Tramp OT 1200, Document DOCD-5242, Best of Blues BoB 8
CP.1066-1 *The Last Dime* (-) **Vo 02712, Cq 8850, ARC 7-04-79;** Old Tramp OT 1200, Down With The Game D 204, Document DOCD-5242

No gtr on *.
Chicago, 18 August 1934
C-9315-A ***All Night Long Blues**** (Bunch) **De 7081**; RST BD-2011, MCA (J) MCA-3538, Ace of Hearts, AH 158, Brunswick (G) 88 001, Brunswick (G) 10 358 [EP], Blues Collection BLU NC 082, Document DOCD-5242, Best of Blues BoB 8
C-9316-A ***Numbers Blues*** (Bunch) **De 7082**; Old Tramp OT 1216, Document DOCD-5242, Catfish 121, Catfish 001

Chicago, 23 August 1934
C-9331-A ***Good Home Blues*** (Bunch) **De 7061**; Document DOCD-5242
C-9332-A ***These Times*** (Bunch) **De 7061**; RST BD-2011, MCA (J) MCA-3538, MCA Coral 6.30106, Document DOCD-5242

Acc by his Blue-Blowers: prob Ike Rodgers, tbn; unknown clt, vln; Henry Brown, pno; poss own gtr.
Chicago, 24 August 1934
C-9351-, -A ***Throw Me In The Alley*** (Bunch) **De 7018**; Saydisc SDR191, Origin OJL20, Blues Collection BLU NC 082, Document DOCD 5104, Document DOCD-5242, Catfish 121, Fremeaux FA-255, Old Hat CD 1003
NOTE: Reverse of De 7018 is by Tee McDonald.

Acc by own pno-1; or own gtr-2.
Chicago, 7 September 1934
CP-1112-1 ***C And A Train Blues***-1 (Bunch) **Vo 02810**; Document DOCD-5242
CP-1113-2 ***Last Week Blues***-1 (Bunch) **Vo 02843**; Old Tramp OT 1216, Document DOCD-5242
CP-1114-2 ***Keyhole Blues***-2 (Jordon) **Vo 02843**; Document DOCD-5242
CP-1115-1 ***Long Time Ago*** Blues-2 (Bunch) **Vo 02810**; Old Tramp OT 1216, Document DOCD-5242

Acc by own pno; prob Charlie McCoy, gtr.
Chicago, 11 September 1934
C-9443-A ***Doin' The Best I Can*** (Bunch) **De 7007**; Document DOCD-5321
C-9443-B ***Doin' The Best I Can*** (Bunch) **De 7007**; Saydisc SDR191, Document DOCD-5242, Catfish 121
NOTE: Reverse of De 7007 is by Jimmie Gordon.

Acc by own pno; Casey Bill Weldon, stl gtr; poss Teddy Darby, gtr-1.
Chicago, 25 March 1935
C-921-A ***The Rising Sun Blues*** (Bunch) **Vo 03066, Cq 9028**; Saydisc SDR191, Document DOCD-5242
C-922-B ***Blues At My Door*** (Bunch) **Vo 02942, Cq 9027**; Document DOCD-5242
C-923-B ***Truthful Blues (Tell Me The Truth)*** (Bunch) **Vo 02942, Cq 9027**; Document DOCD-5242
C-924-A ***Good Whiskey Blues***-1 (Bunch) **Vo 02978, Cq 8875, ARC 7-05-62**; Old Tramp OT 1216, CBS (UK) 66218, Proper PROPERBOX7, Document DOCD-5242

Chicago, 26 March 1935

C-943-B *More Good Whiskey Blues*-1 (Wheatstraw) **Vo 03119, Cq 8858**;RST BD-2011, Down With The Game D 204, Columbia 67002, P-Vine 2772/75, Document DOCD-5242, Fremeaux FA-255

C-944-A *Letter Writing Blues*-1 (-) **Vo 02978, Cq 8875, ARC 7-05-62**; Saydisc SDR191, Document DOCD-5242

Acc by own pno.

Chicago, 17 July 1935

90167-A *Whiskey Head Blues* (Bunch) **De 7111**; Document DOCD-5242, Catfish 121

90168-A *Slave Man Blues* (Bunch) **De 7111**; Document DOCD-5242, Fremeaux FA-255, Habana JBM 111800

90169-A *C And A Train Blues* (Bunch) **De 7123**; Document DOCD-5242

90170-A *Good Hustler Blues* (Bunch) **De 7123**; Document DOCD-5243

90173-A *Cocktail Man Blues* (Bunch-Smith) **De 7144**; Saydisc SDR19, Document DOCD-5243

90174-A *King Spider Blues* (Bessie Smith) **De 7144**; Saydisc SDR191, Document DOCD-5243

Acc by own pno; poss Charlie Jordan, gtr.

Chicago, 20 July 1935

C-1078-A *Hi-De-Ho Woman Blues* (Smith) **Vo 03035, Cq 9767**; Document DOCD-5243

C-1079-A *Sorrow Hearted Blues* (Smith) **Vo 03119, Cq 8858**; Old Tramp OT 1216, Document DOCD-5243

C-1080-A *Up The Road Blues* (Bunch) **Vo 03035**; Document DOCD-5243

C-1081-B *Last Dime Blues* (Bunch) **Vo 03444**; Saydisc SDR191, Document DOCD-5243

C-1082-B *King Of Spades* (Smith) **Vo 03066, Cq 9028**; Saydisc SDR191, Document DOCD-5243

C-1083-A *Johnnie Blues* (Smith) **Vo 03155**; Old Tramp OT 1200, Document DOCD-5243, Fremeaux FA-255

Chicago, 31 October 1935

90416-A *Santa Claus Blues* (Jordon-Bunch) **De 7129**; RST BD-2011, Sunflower ET-1402, Document DOCD-5243

90417-A *Lonesome Lonesome Blues* (Bunch) **De 7129**; RST BD-2011, Sunflower ET-1402, Document DOCD-5243

Duet with Bumble Bee Slim; acc by own pno.

Chicago, 7 February 1936

90614-A *No Good Woman (Fighting Blues)* (Easton-Bunch) **De 7170**; Document DOCD-5243

NOTE Reverse of De 7170 is by Bumble Bee Slim.

Acc by own pno; unknown gtr.

Chicago, 13 February 1936

C-1257-2 *First And Last Blues* (Bunch) **Vo 03185**; Saydisc SDR191, Document DOCD-5243

C-1258-1 *True Blue Woman* (Bunch) **Vo 03185**; Saydisc SDR191, Document DOCD-5243

C-1259-2 *Kidnapper's Blues* (Bunch) **Vo 03249, Cq 8925, ARC 7-07-66**; Document DOCD-5243, Body & Soul 3043912
C-1260-2 *Working Man* Vo unissued
C-1261-1 *Sweet Home Blues* (Bunch) Columbia (US) 46215, Document DOCD-5243
C-1261-2 *Sweet Home Blues* (Bunch) **Vo 03396**; Saydisc SDR191, Document DOCD-5243
C-1262.-1 *Good Woman Blues* (Bunch) **Vo 03396**; RST BD-2011, RBF RF-12, Document DOCD-5243

Acc by own pno; Kokomo Arnold, gtr.

New York, 18 February 1936
60506-A *Working Man (Doin' The Best Can)* (Bunch) **De 7200**; Blues Classics BC 4, Document DOCD-5243, Fremeaux FA-255, Indigo 2040
60507-A *Low Down Rascal* (Bunch-Smith) **De 7200**; Saydisc SDR 192, Document DOCD 5243
60511-A *When I Get My Bonus (Things Will Be Coming My Way)* (Bunch) **De 7159**; Saydisc SDR192, Document DOCD-5243
60512-A *Coon Can Shorty* (Jordan) **De 7159**; Saydisc SDR192, Document DOCD-5243, Catfish 121

New York, 19 February 1936
60522-A *Meat Cutter Blues* (Smith) **De 7187**; RST BD-2011, MCA (J) MCA-3538, Document DOCD-5243, Best of Blues BoB 8
60523-A *The First Shall Be Last And The Last Shall Be First* (William Bunch) **De 7167**; Saydisc SDR192, Document DOCD-5243
60527-A *Kidnappers Blues* (Jordan) **De 7177**, Old Tramp OT 1200, MCA (J) 3538, Document DOCD-5243, Catfish 121, Fremeaux FA-255

New York, 20 February 1936
60532-A *Old Good Whiskey Blues* (Jordan) **De 7187**; Old Tramp OT 1200, Document DOCD-5244
60538-A *Poor Millionaire Blues* (Smith Bunch) **De 7177**; Old Tramp OT 1216, Document DOCD-5461
60539-A *Deep Sea Love* (William Bunch) **De 7167**; Saydisc SDR192, Document DOCD-5244
60540-A *Drinking Man Blues* (Muldron Bunch) **De 7228**; RST BD-2011, MCA (J) MCA-3538, Best of Blues BoB 8, Blues Collection BLU NC 082, Document DOCD-5244

New York, 21 February 1936
60544-A *Country Fool Blues* (Bessie Smith) **De 7228**; Old Tramp 1216, Document DOCD-5244

Acc by own pno; various unknown gtrs.

Chicago, 8 April 1936
C-1348-2 *Jungle Man Blues* (Bunch) **Vo 03231**; Old Tramp OT 1200, Document DOCD-5244
C-1349-1 *Santa Fe Blues* (Bunch) **Vo 03231**; Old Tramp OT 1200, Document DOCD-5244
C-1350-2 *Mistreated Love Blues* (Harrison) **Vo 03273, Cq 8859, ARC 7-06-58**; Document DOCD-5244

C-1351-2 *Remember And Forget Blues* (Harrison) **Vo 03273, Cq 8859, ARC 7-06-58;** Saydisc SDR192, Document DOCD-5244
C-1352-1 *Don't Take A Chance (Losing A Good Woman)* (Harrison-Bunch) **Vo 03348;** Saydisc SDR192, Document DOCD-5244
C-1353-1 *Froggie Blues* (Harrison) **Vo 03249, Cq 8925, ARC 7-07-66;** Document DOCD-5244

Chicago, 9 April 1936

C-1354-2 *Block And Tackle* (M. Harrison) **Vo 03348;** Saydisc SDR192, Document DOCD-5244
C-1355-1 *Cut Out Blues* (M. Harrison) **Vo 03444;** Saydisc SDR191, Document DOCD-5244

Acc by own pno; Kokomo Arnold, gtr; unknown sbs; unknown gtr replaces Arnold-1.

Chicago, 26 October 1936

90961-A *When A Man Gets Down*-1 (Bunch) **De 7243;** Saydisc SDR192, Document DOCD-5244
90962-A *I Don't Want No Pretty Faced Woman*-1 (Harriston) **De 7257;** Old Tramp OT 1200, Document DOCD-5244
90963-A *False Hearted Woman* (Bunch) **De 7243;** Saydisc SDR192, Document DOCD-5244
90964-A *Little House (I'm Gonna Chase These Peppers)* (Bunch) **De 7257;** Old Tramp OT 1200, Best of Blues BoB 8, Document DOCD-5244, Catfish 121
90965-A *Fairasee Woman (Memphis Woman)* (Harriston) **De 7272;** RST BD-2011, Sunflower ET-1402, Document DOCD-5244
90966-A *Beggar Man Blues* (Harriston-Bunch) **De 7272;** RST BD-2011, Sunflower ET-1402, Document DOCD-5244, Fremeaux FA-255

Acc by own pno; unknown gtr; sbs.

Chicago, 26 March 1937

91150-A *Crazy With The Blues* (Bunch-Jordan) **De 7348;** Decca DL 4434, RST BD-2011, MCA 3-11441, Blues Collection BLU NC 082, Document DOCD-5244
91151-A *Ramblin' Man* (Bunch-Jordan) **De 7348;** Document DOCD-5244
91152-A *Peetie Wheatstraw Stomp* (Bunch) **De 7292;** Blues Classics BC4, Albatros (I) VPA-8456, Document DOCD-5244, Document DOCD 32-20-2, Blues Collection BLU NC 082, Smithsonian RD101-3, Catfish 121, Fremeaux FA-255, Fremeaux 033 36, Disky 247282, ZYX/Nostalgia 006
91153-A *Peetie Wheatstraw Stomp No.2* (Bunch) **De 7391;** Blues Classics BC4, Document DOCD-5244, Catfish 121, Fremeaux FA-255
91154-A *Crapshooter's Blues* (Bunch) **De 7292;** Saydisc SDR192, Document DOCD-5245
91155-A *Would You Would You Mama* (Bunch) **De 7311;** Best of Blues BoB 10, White label VJBR8, Best of Blues BoB 8, Document DOCD-5245

Acc by own pno; KokomoArnold, gtr.

Chicago, 30 March 1937

91163-A *Give Me Black Or Brown* (Jordan) **De 7391;** Document DOCD-5245

91164-A *Working On The Project* (Jordan) **De 7311**; Blues Classics BC4; Blues Collection BLU NC 082, Document DOCD-5245, Catfish 121, Fremeaux FA-255

Acc by own pno; unknown gtr, sbs.

Chicago, 2 November 1937

91317-A *Sick Bed Blues* (Bunch) **De 7403**; Saydisc SDR192, Document DOCD-5245
91320-A *I'm Gonna Cut Out Everything* (Jordan-Bunch) **De 7422**; Saydisc SDR192, Document DOCD-5245
91321-A *New Working On The Project* (Jordan) **De 7379**; Old Tramp 1200, Document DOCD-5245
91322-A *Baby Lou, Baby Lou* (Jordan-Bunch) **De 7403**; Document DOCD-5245
91323-A *Devilment Blues* (Jordan) **De 7422**; Saydisc SDR192, Document DOCD-5245
91324-A *Third Street's Going Down* (Jordan) **De 7379**; RST BD-2011, Mamlish S-3806, Swingtime BT 2017, MCA (J) MCA-3538, Blues Collection BLU NC 082, Document DOCD-5245, Catfish 121

Acc by own pno; Lonnie Johnson, gtr; unknown sbs; unknown dms-l.

New York, 1 April 1938

63535-B *304 Blues (Lost My Job On The Project)* (Jordan) **De 7453**; Document DOCD-5245, Catfish 121
63536- *The Wrong Woman* (Jordan-Bunch) **De 7465**; Old Tramp OT 1216, Document DOCD-5245
63537-B *Hard Headed Black Gal* (Giles Jones) **De 7453**; Document DOCD-5245, Catfish 121
63538-A *Banana Man* (Giles Jones) **De 7465**; DOCD-5245, Fremeaux FA-255
63539-A *Shack Bully Stomp*-1 (Giles Jones) **De 7479**; Blues Classics BC4, Magpie PY 4413, MCA (J) MCA-3521-3522, Blues Collection BLU NC 082, Document DOCD-5245, Catfish 121, Fremeaux FA-255, Blues Collection EPM 15839-2, Classic Blues CBL 200004, Columbia River 1118, Columbia River 312009, Columbia River 12006, Disky 247282, Star Sounds 3711-2
63540-B *Road Tramp Blues* (Giles Jones) **De 7589**; Blues Classics BC4; Brunswick 87.504, Albatros VPA 8189, Albatros ALB 8, Document DOCD-5245
63541-A *Sweet Lucille* (Jordan-Bunch) **De 7441**; Document DOCD-5245
63542-A *Saturday Night Blues* (Gordon Bunch) **De 7498**; Document DOCD-5245
63544-A *Good Little Thing* (Jordan Bunch) **De 7498**; Document DOCD-5245
63545-A *Cake Alley* (Jordan-Bunch) **De 7441**; Document DOCD-5245, Blues Collection BLU NC 082, Catfish 121, Fremeaux FA-255
63546-A *What More Can A Man Do?*-1 (Jordon) **De 7479**; RST BD-2011, MCA (J) MCA-3526, MCA (J) VIM-20/21/22, Document DOCD-5245, Fremeaux FA-255, Habana JBM 111800

Acc by own pno; Lonnie Johnson, gtr; unknown dms.

Chicago, 18 October 1938

91525-A *Truckin' Thru Traffic* (Jordan) **De 7529**; Saydisc SDR192, MCA 3-11441, Document DOCD-5245, Catfish 121

91526-A *Hot Spring Blues (Skin And Bones)* (Jordan-Bunch) **De 7544**; Document DOCD-5245, Fremeaux FA-255
91527-A *A Man Ain't Nothin' But A Fool* (Jordon-Bunch) **De 7568**; Document DOCD-5245
91528-A *Black Horse Blues* (Jordon-Bunch) **De 7568**; Old Tramp OT 1200, Document DOCD-5246, Fremeaux FA-255
91529-A *Sugar Mama* (Jordan-Bunch) **De 7529**; Saydisc SDR192, Document DOCD-5246, Fremeaux FA-255
91530-A *Me No Lika You* (Jordan-Bunch) **De 7544**; Document DOCD-5246, Fremeaux FA-255

Acc by Sam Price, pno; Teddy Bunn, gtr-l; O'Neil Spencer, dms.
New York, 30 March 1939
65310-A *Possum Den Blues* (Bunch-Jordan) **De 7589**; DOCD-5246, Wolf WBJ CD 007
65310-B *Possum Den Blues* (Bunch-Jordan) **De 7589**; DOCD-5246, Wolf WBJ CD 007
65311-A *Little Low Mellow Mama*-1 (Jordan) **De 7578**; Best of Blues BoB 10, White label VJBR8, Best of Blues BoB 8, Document DOCD-5246
65312-A *A Working Man's Blues*-1 (Jordan) **De 7641**; Document DOCD-5246, Wolf WBJ CD 007
65313-A *One To Twelve (Just As Show)*-1 (Bunch) **De 7605**; Old Tramp OT 1200, Best of Blues BoB 8, Document DOCD-5246
65314-A *Let's Talk Things Over*-1 (William Bunch) **De 7605**; Old Tramp OT 1200, Document DOCD-5246
65315-A *Sinking Sun Blues*-1 (Bunch) **De 7578**; Best of Blues BoB 10, White label VJBR8, Best of Blues BoB 8, Document DOCD-5246
65316-A *Easy Way Blues*-1 (Jordan) **De 7641**; Document DOCD-5246, Wolf WBJ CD 007
65317-A *Machine Gun Blues*-1 (Jordan) **De 7778**; Document DOCD-5246, Wolf WBJ CD 007

Acc by unknown pno; prob Lonnie Johnson, gtr; unknown dms; Rhythm Willie [Hood], hca-l.
Chicago, 14 September 1939
91775-A *Beer Tavern* (Jordan) **De 7657**; Document DOCD-5246, Fremeaux FA-255
91776-A *You Can't Stop Me From Drinking* -1 (Jordan) **De 7692**; Best of Blues BoB 10, White label VJBR8, Best of Blues BoB 8, Gallerie 436, Document DOCD-5246, Digimode CLB 47504
91777-A *I Want Some Sea Food*-1 (Jordan) **De 7657**; RST BD-2011, MCA (J) MCA-3538, Document DOCD-5246, Fremeaux FA-255
91778-A *Rolling Chair*-1 (Jordan) **De 7676**; Document DOCD-5246, Fremeaux FA-255
91779-A *Love Bug Blues*-1 (Jordan) **De 7676**; RST BD-2011, Brunswick (G) 88 001, Brunswick (G) 10 358 [EP], Document DOCD-5246, Fremeaux FA-255
91780-A *Confidence Man*-1 (Jordan) **De 7692**; Best of Blues BoB 10, White label VJBR8, Best of Blues BoB 8, Document DOCD-5246, Fremeaux FA-255

Acc by Jonah Jones, tpt; Lil Armstrong, pno; Sid Catlett, dms.

New York, 4 April 1940

67481-A *Big Apple Blues* (Jordan) **De 7753**; Document DOCD-5246
67482-A *Big Money Blues* (Jordan) **De 7738**; Best of Blues BoB 10, White label VJBR8, Best of Blues BoB 8, Document DOCD-5246
67483-A *Chicago Mill Blues* (Jordan) **De 7788**; RST BD-2011, Albatros VPA 8473, Brunswick (G) 10 358 [EP], Bella Musica (G) BM-3023, Document DOCD-5246, Catfish 121, Fremeaux FA-255
67484-A *Five Minutes Blues* (Jordan-Bunch) **De 7738**; Best of Blues BoB 10, White label VJBR8, Best of Blues BoB 8, Document DOCD-5246
67485-A *Two Time Mama* (Bunch-Jordan) **De 7753**; Document DOCD-5246
67486-A *Jaybird Blues* (Jordan) **De 7798**; Best of Blues BoB 10, White label VJBR8, Decca (US) DL-79230, MCA (US) MCA-1353, Best of Blues BoB 8, Document DOCD-5247
67487-A *Suicide Blues* (Jordan) **De 7788**; Best of Blues BoB 10, White label VJBR8, Best of Blues BoB 8, Document DOCD-5247, Fremeaux FA-255
67488-A *Pocket Knife Blues* (Jordan) **De 7778**; Best of Blues BoB 10, Decca (US) DL-79230, Best of Blues BoB 8, Document DOCD-5247

New York, 28 August 1940

68022-A *Gangster's Blues* (Luther-Williams) **De 7815**; RST BD-2011, Albatros VPA 8474, Brunswick (G) 10 358 [EP], Blues Collection BLU NC 082, Document DOCD-5247, Catfish 121, Fremeaux FA-255, Columbia River 312011
68023-A *Cuttin' 'Em Slow* (Williams) **De 7798**; Best of Blues BoB 10, White label VJBR8, Best of Blues BoB 8, Document DOCD-5247
68024-A *Look Out For Yourself* (Williams) **De 7815**; Best of Blues BoB 10, White label VJBR8, Best of Blues BoB 8, Document DOCD-5247
68025-A *No 'Count Woman* (Williams) **De 7823**; Best of Blues BoB 10, White label VJBR8, Best of Blues BoB 8, Document DOCD-5247
68026-A *What's That?* (Bunch-Jordan) **De 7823**; Best of Blues BoB 10, White label VJBR8, MCA (J) MCA-3539, Best of Blues BoB 8, Document DOCD-5247, Fremeaux FA-255

Acc by poss Lil Armstrong, pno; Robert Lee McCoy, hca.

Chicago, 12 March 1941

93585-A *I Don't Feel Sleepy* (Oden) **De 7837**; Best of Blues BoB 10, White label VJBR8, Best of Blues BoB 8, Document DOCD-5247, Fremeaux FA-255
93586-A *My Little Bit* (Oden) **De 7837**; Best of Blues BoB 10, White label VJBR8, Best of Blues BoB 8, Document DOCD-5247, Fremeaux FA-255
93587-A *Seeing Is Believing* (Oden) **De 7857**; Best of Blues BoB 10, White label VJBR8, Best of Blues BoB 8, Document DOCD-5247
93588-A *The Good Lawd's Children* (Williams) **De 7879**; Document DOCD-5247
93589-A *You Got To Tell Me Something* (Williams) **De 7844**; Old Tramp OT 1200, Document DOCD-5247
93590-A *Love Me With Attention* (Williams) **De 7844**; Old Tramp OT 1200, Document DOCD-5247, Catfish 121, Fremeaux FA-255

93591-A *I'm A Little Piece Of Leather* (Williams) **De 7857**; Best of Blues BoB 10, White label VJBR8, Best of Blues BoB 8, Document DOCD-5247

Acc by unknown ten-l; poss Lil Armstrong or Jack Dupree, pno; unknown sbs.

Chicago, 25 November 1941

93843-A *Don't Put Yourself On The Spot* (Green) **De 7894**; Document DOCD-5247
93844-A *Old Organ Blues*-l (Green) **De 7901**; Document DOCD-5247, Fremeaux FA-255
93845-A *Hearse Man Blues*-l (Oden) **De 7886**; RST BD-2011, Sunflower ET-1402, Document DOCD-5247, Fremeaux FA-255
93846-A *Bring Me Flowers While I'm Living*-l (Green-Oden) **De 7886**; RST BD-2011, Sunflower ET-1402, Document DOCD-5247, Fremeaux FA-255
93847-A *Pawn Broker Blues* (Green-Oden) **De 7894**; Document DOCD-5247
93848-A *Southern Girl Blues* (L. Williams) **De 7904**; Old Tramp OT 1200, Document DOCD-5247
93849-A *Mister Livingood* (L. Williams) **De 7879**; Document DOCD-5247
93850- *The Good Lawd's Children* De unissued
93851- *Separation Day Blues* (Jordan) **De 7901**; Document DOCD-5247, Catfish 121, Fremeaux FA-255
NOTE: Reverse of De 7904 is by Oscar Woods.

Titles of LPs, EPs and CDs that appear in the Discography

Ace of Hearts (UK) AH158 = Out Came The Blues Vol. 2
Albatros (I) ALB 8 = Il Blues Rurale/Jazzistico/Urbano
Albatros (I) VPA 8189 = Il Blues Urbano/Urban Blues
Albatros (I) VPA-8456 = Erotic Blues
Albatros (I) VPA-8473 = Big City Blues
Albatros (I) VPA 8474 = Combo Blues
Bella Musica (I) BM-3023 = The Blues Pioneers
Best of Blues (Au) BoB 8 = Peetie Wheatstraw (1931-1941)
Best of Blues (Au) BoB10 = Peetie Wheatstraw (1937-1941)
Bluebird (US) 09026-63988-2 That's Chicago's South Side. When the Sun Goes Down. The Secret History of Rock and Roll, Vol. 3.
Blues Classics (US) 4 = Kokomo Arnold / Peetie Wheatstraw
Blues Collection (UK) BLU NC 082 = The Devil's Son-in-Law
Blues Collection (F) EPM 15839 2 = Saint Louis Blues (1925-41)
Body & Soul (F) 3043912 = Blues: La Grande Anthologie 1925-1962
Brunswick (G) 88 001 = The Best of "This Is The Blues"
Brunswick (G) 10 358 [EP] = This Is The Blues Vol.8
Brunswick (G) 87504 = Bad Luck Blues
Catfish (UK) 001 = 20th Century Blues
Catfish (UK) 107 = Beg, Borrow or Steal: the Origins, Music and Influence of Robert Johnson
Catfish (UK) 121 = Peetie Wheatstraw: The Last Straw
CBS (UK) 52797 = Recording The Blues
CBS (UK) 66218 = Story of the Blues (Double LP)
Charly (UK) CD DIG 18 = Good Morning Blues A Classic Blues Anthology 1920-1942

Classic Blues (UK) CBL 200004 Piano Blues The Essential:
Columbia (US) 46215 = Legends of the Blues Volume I
Columbia (US) C4K 47911 = Roots n' Blues: The Retrospective
Columbia (US) CK 67002 = Roots n' Blues: Booze & the Blues
Columbia River 118 = Blues Hits
Columbia River 12006 = Blues Hits, Volume 1
Columbia River 312009 = Blues Suite
Columbia River 312011 = Men of Blues
Decca (US) DL-4434 = Out Came the Blues
Decca (US) DL-79230 = The Blues and All That Jazz
Digimode CLB 47504 = The Story of the Blues #4
Disky (N) 247282 = As Good As It Gets—Jukebox Blues
Document (Au) DOCD-5104 = St. Louis Barrelhouse Piano
Document (Au) DOCD-5241 = Peetie Wheatstraw Complete Recorded Works in Chronological Order, Volume 1, 1930-1932
Document (Au) DOCD-5242 = Peetie Wheatstraw Complete Recorded Works in Chronological Order, Volume 2, 25 March 1934 to 17 July 1935
Document (Au) DOCD-5243 = Peetie Wheatstraw Complete Recorded Works in Chronological Order, Volume 3, 17 July 1935 to 19 February 1936
Document (Au) DOCD-5244 = Peetie Wheatstraw Complete Recorded Works in Chronological Order, Volume 4, 20 February 1936 to 26 March 1937
Document (Au) DOCD-5245 = Peetie Wheatstraw Complete Recorded Works in Chronological Order, Volume 5, 26 March 1937 to 18 October 1938
Document (Au) DOCD-5246 = Peetie Wheatstraw Complete Recorded Works in Chronological Order, Volume 6, 18 October 1938 to 4 April 1940
Document (Au) DOCD-5247 = Peetie Wheatstraw Complete Recorded Works in Chronological Order, Volume 7, 4 April 1940 to 25 November 1941
Document(Au) DOCD-5321 = Too Late, Too Late - Vol. 4
Document (Au) DOCD-5461 = Too Late, Too Late - Vol 6
Document (UK) DOCD-32-20-2 = Bill Wyman's Blues Odyssey
Down With The Game (UK) D 204 = Vintage Country Blues vol.4 "Walter and Peetie"
Fremeaux (F) FA 255 = Peetie Wheatstraw. The Blues: Saint Louis - Chicago - New York 1931-1941
Fremeaux (F) 033 36 = Masterpieces of Blues
Gallerie 436 = Portrait of Vintage Blues
Habana JBM (F) 111800 = Les Triomphes du Blues
Indigo (UK) IGOCD 2040 = I Need A Shot
Indigo (UK) IGOCD 2076 = Hear Me Talkin'
Magpie (UK) PY 4413 = Piano Blues Vol. 13 Central Highway 1933-41
Mamlish (US) S-3805 = Good Time Blues; St Louis 1926-1932
Mamlish (US) S-3806 = Hard Times Blues St Louis 1933-1940.
MCA (US) MCAD 3-11441 = Blues Classics
MCA (G) Coral 6.30106 = Blues Box 1
MCA (US) MCA-1353 = Blues and All That Jazz 1937-47
MCA (J) 3521/2 = Blues, Boogie and Beat
MCA (J) 3526 = Blues in the 30s
MCA (J) 3537 = Juke Joint Blues Piano

MCA (J) 3538 = Charley Jordan / Peetie Wheatstraw
MCA (J) 3539 = Bawdy Blues 1935-1940
MCA (J) VIM 20/21/22 [3 lp set]
Old Hat (US) CD-1003 = Folks He Sure Do Pull Some Bow: Vintage Fiddle Music 1927-1935
Old Tramp (H) 1200 = Peetie Wheatstraw (1931-1941)
Old Tramp (H) 1216 = Peetie Wheatstraw, Volume 2 (1930-1938)
Origin (US) OJL20 = Blues In St. Louis 1929-1937
P-Vine (J) 2772/75 = The Story of Pre-War Blues
P-Vine (J) 5728 = Peetie Wheatstraw, the Devil's Son-in-Law (forthcoming)
Pigmeat (UK) PM 002 Country Blues Hard Hitters: "How You Want It Done?"
Proper (UK) PROPERBOX7, "Black, Broke And Blue: An Anthology of Blues Classics and Rarities."
RCA (F) PM 42039 = Blues
RCA Victor (J) RA-5433/5 (or 9051/3) = Blues 1920-1940
RBF (US) RF-12 = Piano Blues
RST(Au) BD-2011= Peetie Wheatstraw (1930-1941)
Saydisc (UK) SDR 191 = Peetie Wheatstraw, the Devil's Son-in-Law
Saydisc (UK) SDR 192 = Peetie Wheatstraw, the High Sheriff of Hell
Star Sounds 3711-2 = Full Spectrum Blues
Sunflower (UK) ET-1402 = Blues Is My Companion
Swingtime (Dk) BT 2017 = Times Are Tight
White Label (Eu) VJBR 8 = Peetie Wheatstraw
Wolf (Au)WSE 115 = St. Louis Blues (1929-1933)
Wolf (Au) WSE 118 = J D. Short, 1930-1933
Wolf (Au) WBJ-007 Sammy Price & The Blues Singers 1929-1950
Yazoo (US) 1030 = St. Louis Blues 1929-1935: The Depression.
Yazoo (US) 2061 = 21st Street Stomp
ZYX Nostalgia (G) 006 = Rock & Roll Boogie

Report of the Bureau of Census 1920—Population. Sheet No. 14A. Freeman township. February 4-6 1920.

INDEX

304 Blues, 82; lyrics, 76
Ain't It A Pity and a Shame: lyrics, 18
Alexander, Texas, 80
All Alone Blues, 24
All Night Long Blues, 29
Altheimer, Joshua, 46
Arhoolie (Label), 110
Armstrong, Lil, 89, 95, 100–101
Armstrong, Louis, 80
Arnold, Kokomo, 12, 38, 92, 110; accompanies Wheatstraw, 46, 65, 74, 116
Attaway, William, 61
Baby Lou, Baby Lou, 77
Back Door Blues, 26
Baker, Houston: on Ralph Ellison, 61
Banana Man, 82
Barbee, John Henry: influence of Wheatstraw on, 56
Barker, Danny: on "Shack Bully", 85
Barrel House Mojo (Iva Smith), 115
Beer Tavern, 94
Beggar Man Blues, 67
Big Apple Blues: lyrics, 96
Big Money Blues, 96
Black Horse Blues: lyrics, 86
Blackwell, Scrapper, 116
Block And Tackle: lyrics, 53
Blues At My Door: lyrics, 38
Blues lyrics: analysis of, 85; and desire, 85; as revelatory of character, 1, 73
Brewer, Blind James: on Wheatstraw's musical ability, 5
Bring Me Flowers While I'm Living: lyrics, 105
Brooklyn, Illinois, 7
Broonzy, Big Bill, 37
Brown, Henry, 5
Bumble Bee Slim. *See* Easton, Amos
Bunch, Sam (brother): meeting, 113
Bunn, Teddy, 89
C and A. *See* Chicago and Alton Railroad
C And A Blues, 19
C And A Train Blues, 32; lyrics, 30
C And A Train Blues (3rd version), 39

Cabin Inn (Club), 58
Cake Alley: lyrics, 83
Cake Alley (locale in St. Louis), 84
Can't See Blues, 24
Carr, Leroy, 5, 116; influence of, 58
Carter, Spider, 12
Catfish (Label), 111
Catlett, Sid, 95
Chicago and Alton Railroad (C and A), 32
Chicago Mill Blues: lyrics, 96
Cocktail Man Blues, 39
Communist Party of the United States (CPUSA): position on African American issues, 61
composer credits, 12–13
Confidence Man: lyrics, 94
Coon Can Shorty, 47
Cotton Plant, Arkansas, 3, 109; burial of Wheatstraw in, 114; researchers visiting, 113-114
.Council, Floyd "Dipper Boy": influence of Wheatstraw on, 57
Country Fool Blues, 48
Crapshooter's Blues: lyrics, 69
Crazy With The Blues, 56, 64; lyrics, 68; possible reference to suicide in, 98
Crazy With The Blues (Lazy Bill Lucas), 56
Cut Out Blues, 77; lyrics, 55
Cuttin' 'Em Slow, 99
CWA (Civil Works Administration), 76
Darby, Teddy, 7, 24, 37; on death of Wheatstraw, 106; on Wheatstraw's never holding a regular job, 95; on Wheatstraw's musical ability, 5
Davis, Walter, 5, 58, 116
DeBerry, James: influence of Wheatstraw on, 56
Deep Sea Love, 46
Deep Water Blues (Jazz Gillum), 57
Devil, the, 115; Peetie Wheatstraw and, 114
The *Devil's Daddy-in-Law*. *See* Council, Floyd "Dipper Boy"

Devil's Son-in-Law: as a character, 23, 115
"The Devil's Son-in-Law": first appears on record label, 16
Devil's Son-in-Law, 22; lyrics, 23
Devilment Blues, 77
Direction (magazine), 61
Doin' The Best I Can: lyrics, 33
Don't Feel Welcome Blues, 15; lyrics, 16
Don't Hang My Clothes on No Barb Wire Line: lyrics, 18
Don't Put Yourself On The Spot, 101
Don't Take A Chance, 53
Down With The Game (label), 110
Dozens, the, 93
Drinking Man Blues: lyrics, 48
Dupree, Jack, 101; influence of Wheatstraw on, 56
East St. Louis: race riot in, 9; reputation of, 9
Easton, Amos, 42, 116
Easy Way Blues, 93
Edwards, David "Honeyboy": on Wheatstraw's personality, 73
Ellington, Duke, 80
Ellison, Ralph, 59-63; and blues, 61; political position of, 61
Fairasee Woman (Memphis Woman), 68; lyrics, 67
False Hearted Woman: lyrics, 66
fantasy: critical role of, 95
FERA (Federal Emergency Relief Administration), 76
Fields, Willie, 14, 15
First And Last Blues, 43
The First Shall Be Last And The Last Shall Be First: lyrics, 46
Five Minutes Blues, 96
Foley, Barbara: on Ralph Ellison, 61
Four O'Clock In The Morning, 14
Fremeaux (Label), 111
Freud, Sigmund, 61
Froggie Blues: lyrics, 53
Gangster's Blues, 100; lyrics, 99
Georgia Slim: influence of Wheatstraw on, 57

Gillum, Jazz: influence of Wheatstraw on, 57
Give Me Black Or Brown, 74
Good Home Blues, 29
Good Hustler Blues, 39
The Good Lawd's Children, 102; lyrics, 100
Good Little Thing, 82
Good Whiskey Blues: lyrics, 36
Good Woman Blues: lyrics, 45
Gordon, Jimmie, 12; influence of Wheatstraw on, 57; records as "Peetie Wheatstraw's Brother", 33
Green, Lee, 5
Hard Headed Black Gal, 82
Harris, Mary, 12
Hearse Man Blues: lyrics, 104
Henderson, Leroy, 12
Hi-De-Ho Woman Blues, 40
"High Sheriff from Hell": first mentioned on record, 32, appears on record label, 46
Hobo jungles, 50
Hogg, Smokey: influence of Wheatstraw on, 53, 56, 57
Hot Spring Blues (Skin and Bones): lyrics, 86
House, Son, 114
How Long, How Long, Blues (Leroy Carr), 116
Hughes, Langston, 63
Humor in blues, 28
I Don't Feel Sleepy, 100
I Don't Want No Pretty Faced Woman: lyrics, 65
I Want Some Sea Food: lyrics, 94
I'm A Little Piece Of Leather, 100
I'm Gonna Cut Out Everything, 77
Imagination in the blues, 44
imitation and influence, as separate attributes, 57
Invisible Man (Ralph Ellison), 59-63
Jaybird Blues: lyrics, 98
Johnnie Blues: lyrics, 40
Johnson, James "Stump", 5
Johnson, Lonnie, 11, 80, 86, 94
Johnson, Louise, 68

135

Johnson, Robert: and the Devil, 114–15; influence of Wheatstraw on, 56
Johnson, Tommy: and the Devil, 114
Jones, Jonah, 95
Jones, Little Johnnie, 33
Jordan, Charlie, 7, 12, 38, 93; biographical details, 17; photo mistaken for Peetie, 59
Juneteenth (Ralph Ellison), 60
Jungle Man Blues: lyrics, 49
Keyhole Blues, 29
Kidnapper's Blues (Decca), 48
Kidnapper's Blues (Vocalion): lyrics, 43
King, B. B.: influence of Wheatstraw on, 56, 101
King of Spades, 40
King Spider Blues, 56; lyrics, 39
Lang, Eddie, 80
Last Dime Blues, 40
The Last Dime, 26
Last Week Blues: lyrics, 30
Lee, Verdi, 12
Let Me Breathe Thunder (William Attaway), 61
Let's Talk Things Over, 92
Little Bill Gaither ("Leroy's Buddy"), 116
Little House (I'm Gonna Chase These Peppers): lyrics, 67
Little Low Mellow Mama, 92
Lonesome Lonesome Blues: lyrics, 41
Long Lonesome Dive, 98; lyrics, 26
Long Time Ago Blues, 29
Look Out For Yourself, 99
Lord God Stingerroy, 60
Louisville, Kentucky, 7
Love Bug Blues, 94
Love Me With Attention, 100
Low Down Rascal: lyrics, 47
Lucas, Lazy Bill: influence of Wheatstraw on, 56
Machine Gun Blues, 93
Mama's Advice, 18
A Man Ain't Nothing But A Fool, 86
Marx, Karl, 61
McCoy, Charlie, 22, 33

McCoy, Joe, 58
McCoy, Robert Lee, 59, 89, 94, 100
McDonald, Earl, 7
McFarland, Barrelhouse Buck, 12
Me No Lika You, 86
Meat Cutter Blues, 47
Melrose, Lester, 59
Midnight Blues, 26
Mister Livingood, 101; lyrics, 103
Mistreated Love Blues, 52
Moore, Alice, 12
Moore, Rudy Ray, 59
More Good Whiskey Blues, 36; lyrics, 37
Mosely, Walter, 63
Mr Pawn Broker (B. B. King), 56
Murray, Albert, 61
My Baby Blues, 26
My Baby's Worrying Me (Smokey Hogg), 53, 57
My Little Bit, 100
Neckbones. *See* Fields, Willie
The Negro And His Songs (Odum and Johnson), 68
New Challenge (magazine), 61
New Masses (magazine), 61
New Stranger's Blues (Tampa Red), 17
New Working On The Project: lyrics, 74
Nixon, Hammie, 7
No 'Count Woman: lyrics, 99
Numbers Blues: lyrics, 28
O'Meally, Robert, 60
Oden, St. Louis Jimmy, 5
Old Good Whiskey Blues: lyrics, 47
Oliver, Paul, 109
On The Wall (Louise Johnson), 68
One To Twelve: lyrics, 92
Packin' Up Blues, 26
Patton, Charlie, 114
Pawn Broker Blues, 56; lyrics, 101
Peanut the Kidnapper. *See* Sherrill, James
Peetie Wheatstraw Stomp, 115; lyrics, 70
Peetie Wheatstraw Stomp No.2: lyrics, 70

Peetie Wheatstraw's Brother. *See* Gordon, Jimmie
Peetie Wheatstraw's Buddy. *See* Ray, Harmon
Peetie's Boy. *See* McCoy, Robert Lee
Perls, Nick (Yazoo Records), 116
Pete Wheatstraw: lyrics, 22
Petey Wheatstraw, the Devil's Son-in-Law (film, Rudy Ray Moore), 59
Pierson, Leroy, 59
Pocket Knife Blues, 93, 96
poetry: blues as, 23, 39
Police Station Blues: lyrics, 24
Poor Millionaire Blues: lyrics, 48
Possum Den Blues: lyrics, 92
Price, Sam, 89, 93
Prohibition, 35–36
protest: in blues, 23
Race Riot In East St. Louis, July 2,1917 (Elliott Rudwick), 80
Rachell, Yank: on Wheatstraw's personality, 73
Rainey, Ma, 85
Ramblin' Man, 69
Ray, Harmon, 58, 100; on the absence of Wheatstraw's piano on later sessions, 89; career of, 58; photo mistaken for Wheatstraw, 59, 110–11
Remember and Forget Blues, 56; lyrics, 52
Rhythm Willie (Hood), 94
Rising Sun Blues: lyrics, 38
Road Tramp Blues: lyrics, 82
Rolling Chair, 94
Rudwick, Elliott, 80
Rum Cola Blues (Jack Dupree), 56
Santa Claus Blues: lyrics, 41
Santa Fe Blues: lyrics, 52
Saturday Night Blues, 82
Saydisc (label), 110
School Days, 16
Screening The Blues (Paul Oliver), 28
Seeing Is Believing: lyrics, 100
Separation Day Blues: lyrics, 103
Seward, Alec, and Louis Hayes: influenced by Wheatstraw, 57
Shack Bully: defined, 85
Shack Bully Stomp, 116; lyrics, 85

Sherrill, James: influence of Wheatstraw on, 57
Shines, Johnny: influence of Wheatstraw on, 56, 57
Sick Bed Blues, 77
Silver Spade Blues (Peanut the Kidnapper), 57
Sinking Sun Blues: lyrics, 93
Sitting On Top Of The World (Mississippi Sheiks), 33, 99
Six Weeks Old Blues, 56; lyrics, 19
Slave Man Blues, 39
Sleepless Nights Blues, 24
Smith, Bessie, 56
Smith, Iva, 115
So Long Blues, 18
So Soon, 16
Sorrow Hearted Blue, 40
Southern Girl Blues: lyrics, 102
Spaulding, Henry, 84
Spencer, O'Neil, 89, 93
Spider Web Blues (Victoria Spivey), 56
SpiderMan Blues (Bessie Smith), 56
Spivey, Victoria, 56, 80
St. Louis blues scene, 9
St. Louis Jimmy. *See* Oden, St. Louis Jimmy.
Stackhouse, Houston, 7
Stolle, Robert, 113
Strachwitz, Chris (Arhoolie Records), 110
Strange Man Blues, 16; lyrics, 16
Sugar Mama: lyrics, 87
suicide, 98
Suicide Blues: lyrics, 97
Suicide Blues (Peanut the Kidnapper), 57
Suitcase Blues (Smokey Hogg), 57
Sunnyland Slim: on Wheatstraw's reputation in the early 1930s, 5
Superfly (film), 59
Sweet Home Blues: lyrics, 44
Sweet Lucille: lyrics, 83
Sykes, Roosevelt, 5, 17, 46, 58
Tampa Red, 17
Tennessee Peaches Blues: lyrics, 14
These Times, 29

Third Street's Going Down, 80; lyrics, 77
Throw Me In The Alley: lyrics, 29
Townsend, Henry, 24, 46, 73; on blues singers and the police, 11–12; on Robert Lee McCoy, 59; on Wheatstraw as a traveler, 7; on Wheatstraw's musical ability, 3; on Wheatstraw's personality, 73; on Wheatstraw's reputation, 12
Truckin' Thru Traffic, 86
True Blue Woman, 43
Truthful Blues, 38, 39
Two Time Mama, 96
Up The Road Blues, 40
Valley district, 77–78, 80; middle-class view of, 11
Waters, Muddy: influence of Wheatstraw on, 56
Webb, Tommy, 7
Weldon, Casey Bill, 12, 37–38; influence of Wheatstraw on, 57
What More Can A Man Do, 82
What's That?, 99
What's That I Smell (Georgia Tom and Hannah May), 99
Wheatstraw, Peetie: absence of piano on later sessions, 89; as accompanist, 12; address in E. St. Louis, 78; address in St. Louis, 3; attitude toward women, 73; birth of, 3; and blues revival, 109; in census records, 3; composer credits on records of, 12; death of, 106-109; death of foretold in songs of last session, 103; and the Devil, 114; example of music, 25; family of, 3; first records for Decca, 27; first records of, 14; influence of, 33; influence of Leroy Carr on, 5; influence, 56, 58-64 passim;
monotony of later recordings, 89; musical abilities, 5, 24; negative aspects of, 116; others with same name, 64; rattlesnakes, in lyrics, 23, 40, 48; recorded output of, 12; records for Bluebird, 22; records with band, 29, as representative of blues singers, 2; reputation of, 5, 12; self-image, 22–23, 32, 38, 40, 66, 71, 73, 95; social protest in song of, 101; social security application, 3; style, 5, 26, 116; suicide in songs of, 27
Wheatstraw, Peter (Character in *Invisible Man*), 60, 62–63
When A Man Gets Down: lyrics, 65
When I Get My Bonus, 47
Whiskey: effects of, 49
Whiskey Head Blues, 39
White, Bukka, 39; influence of Wheatstraw on, 57
Williams, Big Joe, 7, 24, 37–38; on death of Wheatstraw, 109; influence of Wheatstraw on, 57; on Wheatstraw and Charlie Jordan, 17
Working Man, 44
Working Man Blues (Seward and Hayes): influence of Wheatstraw on, 57
Working Man (Doin' the Best I Can), 47
Working Man (various artists), 33
A Working Man's Blues, 92
Working On The Project: lyrics, 74
Works Progress Administration, 76
Would you Would you Mama: lyrics, 69
WPA. *See* Works Progress Administration
The Wrong Woman, 82
You Can't Stop Me From Drinking, 94
You Got To Tell Me Something, 100

A few words about the
CHARLES H. KERR
Publishing Company

"The Charles H. Kerr Company is a truly extraordinary example of living history. Here is the publisher of Gene Debs, Clarence Darrow, Mother Jones, Mary Marcy, Jack London, Carl Sandburg and hundreds of other outstanding figures—still at it, still fighting the good fight after a hundred glorious years. The American labor movement has a great heritage, and the Charles H. Kerr Company is a precious part of it. It deserves every support."—**Studs Terkel**

"What a remarkable history! How can it ever be estimated, the influ-ence of the Kerr Company over all these years? Above all in this era of communication and the rising of the people all over the world, such a bond with expressions and education of the people must be truly celebrated—more than a statue of liberty: the Kerr Company is a true beacon."—**Meridel LeSueur**

"Charles H. Kerr has a magnificent record . . . . More importantly, it continues that tradition of courageous publishing in these difficult times. Kerr's list of titles provides us with excellent material to continue the fight for a just society."—**Dennis Brutus**

The son of militant abolitionists, Charles Hope Kerr was a libertarian socialist, antiwar agitator, author, translator, vegetarian and scholar. The publishing firm he founded in Chicago in 1886, a few weeks before Haymarket, is today the oldest alternative publishing house in the world. Many books recognized as classics in the fields of labor, socialism, feminism, history, anthropology, economics, civil liberties, animal rights and radical ecology originally appeared under the Charles H. Kerr imprint.

Devoted to publishing controversial books that commercial publishers tend to avoid, the firm has shared the ups and downs of American radicalism. Because of Kerr's outspoken opposition to World War I, many of its publications were suppressed by the U.S. government under the notorious Espionage Act.

At the age of 117, the Kerr Company—a not-for-profit, worker-owned cooperative educational association—is not only a living link with the most vital radical traditions of the past, but also an organic part of today's struggles for social change, peace and justice.

Unlike most other alternative publishers, the Kerr Company has never been subsidized by any political party, never had an "angels," never received any "grants." Our aim today remains what it always has been: to publish books that will help make this planet a good place to live!

As always we need all the help we can get! If *you* would like to help the Charles H. Kerr Company, write today!

Publishers of Anti-Establishment Literature Since 1886
Charles H. Kerr Publishing Company
1740 West Greenleaf Avenue / Chicago, Illinois, 60626

BOOKS FOR A BETTER WORLD

JOE HILL: The IWW & the Making of a Revolutionary Workingclass Counterculture, by Franklin Rosemont. A fresh in-depth study of U.S. labor's most celebrated songwriter & martyr, and the movement he came to exemplify. Over 100 illustrations, including *all* of Hill's cartoons & other art. *"Joe Hill has finally found a chronicler worthy of his revolutionary spirit, sense of humor, and poetic imagination"*—Robin D. G. Kelley. 656 pages. $17.00

IWW SONGS TO FAN THE FLAMES OF DISCONTENT. Facsimile reprint of the classic 1923 edition. All the favorite hobo & protest lyrics by Joe Hill, T-Bone Slim, Ralph Chaplin, Laura Payne Emerson & many more! Songs for picketlines, sit-ins, and demonstrations! 64 pages. $5.00

SOCIALIST & LABOR SONGS OF THE 1930s, edited by Elizabeth Morgan, with a preface by Utah Phillips. 77 great songs of solidarity, revolt, humor & revolution. Large format, with music. 82 pages. $16.00

A HISTORY OF PAN-AFRICAN REVOLT by C. L. R. James, with an Introduction by Robin D. G. Kelley. The classic account of global Black resistance in Africa and the diaspora. 160 pages. $12.00

JUICE IS STRANGER THAN FRICTION: Selected Writings of T-Bone Slim, edited/introduced by Franklin Rosemont. The IWW's greatest "Man of Letters" was an outstanding presurrealist humorist & wordplay genius. *"T-Bone Slim has a lot to tell us, and does it well"*–Noam Chomsky. 160 pages. $10.00

REBEL VOICES: An IWW Anthology, edited with introductions by Joyce L. Kornbluh, with a special introduction by Fred Thompson and "A Short Treatise on IWW Cartoons" by Franklin Rosemont. By far the biggest and best source on IWW history, fiction, songs art and lore. Lavishly illus. 463 pages. $24.00

WHERE ARE THE VOICES? & Other Wobbly Poems by Carlos Cortez, with 20 illustrations by the author, including portraits of Lucy Parsons, Joe Hill, Ben Fletcher & others. Introduction by Archie Green. 64 pages. $10.00

LABOR STRUGGLES IN THE DEEP SOUTH & Other Writings by Covington Hall, edited & introduced by David Roediger. This beautifully illustrated memoir describes many of the finest hours of integrated unionism in the U.S., & the IWW's role in creating unity across racial lines. Includes a selection of Hall's best poems, fables, and articles. 272 pages. $14.00

Please add $3.00 postage for the first item, and fifty cents for each additional item.

CHARLES H. KERR
Est. 1886 / 1740 West Greenleaf Avenue, Chicago, Illinois 60626